To order additional copies of *Joyful Noise,* by Ed Christian, call
1-800-765-6955.

Visit us at www.reviewandherald.com for information on other
Review and Herald® products.

The author may be contacted at christia@kutztown.edu.

Credits:
    Chapters 1-6 are derived from revised versions of two articles, *"The Christian & Rock
Music:* A Review Essay," *Journal of the Adventist Theological Society* [JATS] 13, no. 1 (Spring
2002): 149-183; and "Music for Contemporary Christians: What, Where, and When?"
JATS 13, no. 1 (Spring 2002): 184-209; both copyright © 2002 by Ed Christian.
    Chapter 9 is a revised version of "First Church of the Spiritually Handicapped,"
Adventist Review 179, no. 27 (July 2002; North American Division Edition): 16-21; used
with permission.
    Appendix 1 is a revised version of "Imitating Nina," *Insight,* Dec. 23, 2000, pp. 12,
13; used with permission.
    Appendix 2 is based on "Putting the Word Back in Worship," *Ministry* 74, no. 7 (July
2001): 20, 21, and "Don't Adventists Use the Bible Anymore?" *Adventist Review* 176, no.
20 (May 20, 1999): 8-10; both used with permission.
    Appendix 3 is a revised version of "'Sabbath Is a Happy Day!': What Does Isaiah
58:13-14 Mean?" JATS 13, no. 1 (Spring 2002): 81-90; copyright © 2002 by Ed Christian.
    In all cases the versions in this book are to be considered the approved and corrected
versions.

joyful noise

ed christian

REVIEW AND HERALD® PUBLISHING ASSOCIATION
HAGERSTOWN, MD 21740

The author assumes full responsibility for the accuracy of all facts and quotations
as cited in this book.

Scripture quotations marked NASB are from the *New American Standard Bible,*
copyright © 1960, 1962, 1963, 1968, 1971, 1972, 1973, 1975, 1977, 1994 by the
Lockman Foundation .

Texts credited to NEB are from *The New English Bible.* Copyright © The Delegates
of the Oxford University Press and the Syndics of the Cambridge University Press 1961,
1970. Reprinted by permission.

Texts credited to NIV are from the *Holy Bible, New International Version.*
Copyright © 1973, 1978, 1984, International Bible Society. Used by permission of
Zondervan Bible Publishers.

Texts credited to NKJV are from The New King James Version. Copyright © 1979,
1980, 1982 by Thomas Nelson, Inc. Used by permission. All rights reserved.

Scripture quotations marked NLT are taken from the *Holy Bible,* New Living
Translation, copyright © 1996. Used by permission of Tyndale House Publishers, Inc.,
Wheaton, Illinois 60189. All rights reserved.

Bible texts credited to NRSV are from the Revised Standard Version of the Bible,
copyright © 1989 by the Division of Christian Education of the National Council of the
Churches of Christ in the U.S.A. Used by permission.

Bible texts credited to RSV are from the Revised Standard Version of the Bible,
copyright © 1946, 1952, 1971, by the Division of Christian Education of the National
Council of the Churches of Christ in the U.S.A. Used by permission.

This book was
Edited by Tompaul Wheeler
Copyedited by Jocelyn Fay and James Cavil
Designed by GenesisDesign
Electronic makeup by Shirley M. Bolivar
Cover photo by Kent Barker/The Image Bank
Typeset: 12/15 Bembo

PRINTED IN U.S.A.

07 06 05 04 03   5 4 3 2 1

R&H Cataloging Service
Christian, Ed, 1953-
    Joyful noise: a sensible look at Christian music.

    1. Church music.   I. Title.

            781.71

ISBN 0-8280-1763-8

Contents

Chapter 1

Where I'm Coming From

O come, let us sing to the Lord;
let us *make a joyful noise* to the rock of our salvation!
Let us *come into his presence* with thanksgiving;
let us *make a joyful noise* to him with *songs of praise!*
—Psalm 95:1, 2, NRSV

What music is appropriate for Christians? What music is appropriate in worship? Is there a difference between music appropriate in church and music appropriate at a youth rally or concert? Is there a difference between lyrics appropriate for congregational singing and lyrics appropriate for a person to sing or listen to in private? Are some types of music inherently inappropriate for evangelism?

These are important questions. Congregations have fought over them and even split over them.[1] The answers given have often alienated young people from the church and even driven them to reject God. Some answers have rejuvenated churches; others have robbed congregations of vitality and shackled the work of the Holy Spirit.

In some churches the great old hymns haven't been heard in years. Other churches came late to the "praise music" wars, and music is still a controversial topic. In such churches, where praise

---

[1] I watched attendance at one large church drop by half over several years when a new minister of music ruled that only "serious music," preferably instrumental and played by professional musicians, could be performed there. Congregational singing was limited to a handful of great anthems. Cowed by this person, the pastor accepted the argument that God could not accept as worship or praise anything imperfect. I know of another church that split in two partly because the pastor insisted on playing his guitar and leading his congregation in a half hour of praise songs every week.

music is found in the church service, it is probably accompanied by a single guitar or piano and sung without a trace of the enthusiasm, joy, emotion, and repetition one hears when it is used in charismatic churches. Many churches prefer to use no praise choruses during the church service, some use nothing but praise choruses, and perhaps the majority use a mixture.

What I call (with a grin) "rock 'n' roll church," where such instruments as drums and the electric guitar and bass are used for the song service, is rare. Even where one finds such services, the singing is sometimes lackluster and attendance sparse, so clearly such services are not the sole answer to tepid worship. Few would consider music the heart of the gospel, but it is still a topic that inspires strong statements and hurt feelings.

What is generally called contemporary Christian music (or CCM) embraces a wide variety of musical styles. What they have in common is that they are contemporary, in some way Christian, and music. CCM includes the work of Ralph Carmichael and the Gaithers. It includes both the gentlest of folk music and the hardest of heavy metal and rap. It includes praise songs, scripture songs, country music, White gospel and Black gospel, jazz and blues, reggae and ska, Celtic music, bluegrass, and much more. What draws the most attention—and the most concern—is Christian rock of various sorts. The sales are immense, and so is the influence. Some people find this deeply threatening.

In this book I will first share a little about my own Christian pilgrimage and how my own musical tastes have developed. Why? Because if you know where I stand, you'll better understand the perspective from which I see the subject of music for Christians.

Second, I will present a scriptural basis for making decisions about music. Third, I will share, in two chapters, a number of suggestions about how Christians might best use music, whether as entertainment, as worship, or as a combination of the two, and whether personally, in groups, or in the church setting.

My approach is to allow freedom where there is no harm, especially when this builds faith. I will urge toleration of all differences that are not sinful and recognition that differences in taste or practice are not necessarily sinful. However, I will also uphold the need for congregational unity and consideration of the "weak brother" (1 Cor. 8).

Fourth, I will review, in two chapters, a recent book that has caused a lot of discussion—*The Christian & Rock Music*—and explain why I think its many serious problems keep it from being a sound basis for a Christian approach to music. Fifth, in light of recent books urging Christian musicians to move into the mainstream musical world, I will explain why CCM is also necessary.

The main part of the book concludes with a chapter on my dream of what it should be like when God's people gather together to worship. Following that are three appendixes, the first dealing with the sort of discipleship that could lead one to find my suggestions about music compelling, and the last two dealing not with music but with other aspects of worship.

Where I'm Coming From

What follows will be better understood if I explain the perspective from which I view the issue. I began listening to rock music in sixth grade. I can still whistle most of the top 40 hits of that year, should I hear their titles.

By the time I was 16 I was playing electric guitar in a band, subscribing to *Rolling Stone* (if my mom got to the mail before I did, she threw the magazine away), and experimenting with drugs. In college and graduate school I listened to rock for hours every day—whenever I was studying or writing or driving or reading. My mind was filled with the music and the words. I couldn't get them out of my head. My actions—or at least my fantasies—were influenced by these words to some extent.

About the time I got married, when I was 28, I began walking with God—or at least toward Him—and I realized the music I listened to was not godly and was holding me back. I began pleading with God to free me from it, if that was His will.

One night I awoke sensing that God had opened the door to freedom if I was willing to walk through it. I spent the rest of the night looking at each record album, looking at the names of the songs and thinking about them, then renouncing them. By morning I had said goodbye to 300 albums.

I consider my deliverance from this music to be supernatural. I can still recall the songs, but I don't choose to, and they aren't running through my head. It should be clear from this confession that if in this essay I speak favorably about Christian rock music or other forms of CCM, it is not because I particularly like or listen to this music myself.

I don't often listen to music of any sort these days—I prefer silence—but when I do, it's usually hymns: choral, a cappella, orchestral, folk, or bluegrass. For me, the great old hymns found in our hymnal have a wonderful ability to focus the mind on God and help one say no to temptation.[2]

I enjoy classical music of many sorts, though I seldom listen to it. I also enjoy some types of jazz and swing, especially clarinet solos, and bluegrass, though I rarely listen to them. I used to love opera, especially Mozart and Verdi, but when I read the librettos in English and discovered their focus on sin, I stopped listening, though I still enjoy the overtures.

I took an instant dislike to praise songs when I first heard them in my church. The primary reason was that they were replacing the hymns I loved—so rich and meaningful to me—with what I saw as simplistic melodies, words, and emotions. The second reason is that I'd heard praise songs sung well, powerfully moving the audience, but never in my own denomination.

---

[2] When thoughts I'd rather avoid enter my head, I often begin whistling a hymn, because that seems to drive out temptation. Because I associate the music with the words, merely humming the melody keeps me close to God. I've also found that the lyrics are often stirring and beautiful. My three-tape collection of 155 hymn lyrics read as poetry is available from American Cassette Ministries (www.americancassette.org or 1-800-233-4450). Wonderful though the melodies may be, they often obscure the beauty of the verse.

However, I've come to understand that praise songs really are what they claim to be: they do praise God, and well. Though I still have a hard time singing them in church, I've come to appreciate the best of them, I no longer fight them, and I enjoy accompanying with my guitar those who sing them.

Because I know what it's like to be virtually addicted to rock 'n' roll music and have its incitements to sin running through my head, for many years I was very much opposed to CCM. Two insights have turned my thinking around.

A few years ago I was invited to speak at a youth conference at the University of North Carolina. Sunday morning, driving home to Pennsylvania, I grew weary of sermon tapes and turned on the radio, looking for some classical music. I was approaching Lynchburg, Virginia, Jerry Falwell country, and just about the only thing on the radio other than rock music was various sorts of contemporary Christian music. I had virtually no knowledge of this music, though I had scoffed at it for years.

I found myself listening to a song. Soon several hours had passed, and God revealed a lesson as important (to me) as Peter's lesson about not calling people unclean in Acts 10, 11.

I realized that while I didn't like this rather sappy music, vaguely country-western, it was sung from the heart. These were songs about struggle and victory, about searching and finding, about turning to God for help over the little things. These weren't hymns. They weren't appropriate for church. But they were Christian songs, whether I liked them or not.

I saw, as if on a screen, homemakers doing their chores, struggling to keep their faces turned to God, struggling to believe, struggling to put meals on the table and keep clothes on the kids. I sensed their radios on, filling their lives with songs I scorned, yet songs that touched them and strengthened their faith.

It's odd how quick we are to call sinful what we simply don't like. May God rebuke those who disparage music that draws people to God, however it may sound. (By this I am merely asking

God to help these people realize the errors of their ways. Perhaps you are praying the same for me at the moment. May God guide us all.)

The next summer my sons Paul and Peter returned from a week at junior camp excited about the camp theme song—a song from a Christian rock CD. (I think it was the Rich Mullins song "Awesome God.") Paul sang it to us in the car. I was astonished that such music was heard at camp. Why would counselors introduce my children to music from which I'd carefully shielded them, not wanting them to have the trouble with rock music I had had?

My first thought was to say, "I do not want you to sing that song again." But I kept my mouth shut, not wanting to have an argument on the way home. I could tell them later.

That night Paul, then 11, came to my bedroom. "Dad," he said, "you know that song we learned at camp? The words really got me thinking, and I decided to recommit myself to God."

I told him I was thrilled, of course, but I could hardly breathe. In my heart I was saying, "Oh, God, I nearly bawled him out for liking a song that brought him to You. Thank You so much for shutting my mouth!" Now 14, Paul dreams of becoming a youth pastor.

We've made a deal: Paul can listen to any music he likes, so long as it's Christian. He listens to Christian rap and Christian punk, and we have wonderful open-hearted conversations about the relative quality of the bands he likes and the effect of their lyrics, and about God and the Bible.

There is nothing I want more than for my children to share eternal life with me. May God rebuke those who turn away these little ones from God and His church because they don't realize God can be praised in any language and with almost any music. As Jesus said, " 'If any of you put a stumbling block before one of these little ones who believe in me, it would be better for you if a great millstone were fastened around your neck and you were drowned in the depth of the sea' " (Matt. 18:6). One of the greatest stumbling blocks for young people seeking God is when their elders condemn what the Bible does not condemn—either explicitly or as a correctly derived principle. To deny this is to deny the clear evidence of conversions and transformed lives.[3] May our teaching be based on evidence, not on our prejudice.

---

[3] Sam Leonor, bass player and vocalist for the band Big Face Grace, writes, "I am a witness to the fact that listeners (and players) of Christian music have and are being humbled by the majesty of God, and they have been and continue to be convicted of His moral claims upon their lives" (personal e-mail, Feb. 11, 2002). Like three other members of his band, Leonor has an M.Div. degree. He is the campus chaplain at La Sierra University. I met him at the youth conference mentioned above. I was at first prejudiced against Leonor, as at the time I was very much against any type of rock music. However, I liked what he said to the students at the conference, and we ended up talking together for a couple hours. I was impressed by his dedication to doing God's will and his commitment to Bible teaching. The shock of meeting a theologically conservative rock star (I'm exaggerating) prepared me, I think, for the insights I received the next day as I drove home listening to CCM on the radio. I thank him for his witness to me and to thousands of young people.

Chapter 2

How Do We Decide?
Bible Principles That Help

Make a joyful noise to God, all the earth;
sing the glory of his name; give to him *glorious praise.*
Say to God, "How awesome are your deeds!
Because of your great power, your enemies cringe before you.
All the earth *worships* you;
they *sing praises to you,*
sing praises to your name."
—Psalm 66:1-4, NRSV

There are those who try to base their principles of music on biblical references to musical instruments and musical performance, most of them in the Old Testament. This approach is less useful than they think.[1] First, there is no reason to think we should restrict ourselves to instruments mentioned there. The ones mentioned are the ones they had to work with, and we simply have more now than they did then.

Some suggest that certain instruments—especially rhythm instruments—are not mentioned in connection with Israel's worship because they were associated with pagan worship or secular entertainment. There is no biblical evidence for this at all, unless one chooses to twist and misread the texts. There is no reason a piano or organ should be considered more acceptable, from a biblical viewpoint, than an electric guitar or bass (though I will provide certain cautions later in this book).

Second, the Israelite Temple services give us little useful guid-

---

[1] See chapters 5 and 6 for more on why this is not a useful approach.

ance on music, because there is only a slight relation between the Temple services and our church services. There were worship services at the Temple, but that was not its primary purpose. The Israelite tabernacle—and later Solomon's Temple—was where God dwelled among his people. He was in some way physically present in the Most Holy Place, and because His holiness would destroy what was sinful, He had to be isolated from His people. This is what the tabernacle was for. It was an isolation chamber. Since God was there, that was where people came to sacrifice and worship.

However, the worship service as we know it did not exist. There were sacrifices on the Sabbath, and in Solomon's Temple there was a choir that sang psalms. But there was no church building in which people met to worship, usually no sermon, no children's story, no congregational singing. (Ezra 10:9 records the people's distress at having to sit in the rain outside the Temple while Ezra called them to repentance. Ezra agreed to postpone his sermon.)

People were not required to come to the Temple on the Sabbath. They were not even required to worship on the Sabbath or say certain prayers, so far as we know from the biblical text, except for a "sacred assembly" in a family setting, the equivalent to family worship (Lev. 23:3, NIV). They rested on the Sabbath in their own homes. I suspect the people devoted part of their time to prayer and thanksgiving, but it seems that few went to the Temple to do that.[2]

---

[2] In the fourth commandment (Ex. 20:8-11) God commands that the Sabbath be kept "holy," but I think the Hebrew word *qodeš* should in this context be translated "separate" rather than "holy." God does not command worship in this commandment, but a ceasing from work (the word Sabbath means "ceasing"). The opposite of work is, not holiness, but not working or separation from work, so "separate" seems more appropriate. The fourth commandment gives as a reason for this ceasing God resting from his work on the seventh day of Creation (Gen 2:3) and blessing the day, not on His declaring it a day on which He is to be worshiped. The Sabbath is thus a blessed and God-mandated day of rest from weekday labor. It is also a wonderful time for God's people to meet to praise Him, but that is not the primary purpose of the day. This is supported by the fact that in the Torah God never commands his people to gather together to worship on the Sabbath at the tabernacle in the generations to come, whereas He does command them to come to the tabernacle to celebrate several feasts. For more on the proper use of the Sabbath, see Appendix 3.

Today both *our bodies* and the believers *as a body* are the Temple of God's Spirit (1 Cor. 6:19; 2 Cor. 6:16). Biblically there is no other Temple on earth for God's people today. Jesus says, "'For where two or three come together in my name, there am I with them'" (Matt. 18:20).

This is a staggering thought. It means the center of holiness is inside us, so we must do our best to keep ourselves separate from things that defile us, not only on the Sabbath, but at all times, whether working or resting. We must approach fellow believers reverently, because God is present inside them. It also means the church building has no special holiness of itself. God is less present in an empty church than in two believers praising God together while working in a sewer.[3] Thus it is paradoxical to ask believers to leave "the sanctuary" if they want to chat, because when they leave the room they take the sanctuary with them.[4]

We have no biblical warrant for treating our place of meeting like the tabernacle was treated. This means the restrictions on the tabernacle may apply to us personally in some ways, but usually in a metaphorical way. (The counsel to offer ourselves as "living sacrifices" [Rom. 12:1, NIV] must also be metaphorical, as only certain pure and unblemished animals could be sacrificed, while we are sinful and physically blemished.) The tabernacle restrictions do not apply to the church building. This is fortunate, because if they did apply we couldn't enter.

---

[3] Paul told his listeners on Mars Hill, "'The God who made the world and everything in it is the Lord of heaven and earth and does not live in temples built by hands'" (Acts 17:24). That includes churches.

[4] This is not to say that when we meet in a place of worship we should do things that distract from our own worship of God or others' worship, or threaten the unity of spirit God desires in His people when they worship Him. We may call the room where the church meets "the sanctuary," but that is merely our own coinage. God does not call it that in the Bible or hallow it. I do not mean to suggest that believers should not meet together. We are urged to do that (Heb. 10:25), and the Sabbath is an excellent time to do it. If we choose to meet in what we call a church, in a building we have dedicated to God (even though He hasn't asked us to), and if we choose to have the order of service we have, that is fine, but that order of service is not ordained by God, and there have been many church services in which the "worship" is tepid or cooler. There is no virtue in gathering together to play dead.

Those who turn to the Hebrew Temple as a model for modern worship, using that to call for the highest level of music and the restriction of instruments, go only partway, when logically they should go the whole way (Gal. 5:12). They should dispose of the organ and piano and use only cymbals, lyres, trumpets, and harps (2 Chron. 5:12; 29:25, 26). There should be no singing of hymns, but only psalms, and no congregational singing, but only singing by a choir—men only—wearing white linen dresses. Of course, the entire choir would also have to be from the tribe of Levi, and they would stand outside while singing, barefoot, even in winter. Indeed, if we feel ourselves bound to the musical methods of the Temple, we ought also to return to offering sacrifices (Rom. 2:17-26 is an especially appropriate warning for those who counsel this return to Temple music).

So is there, then, anything in the Bible that can guide us as we consider what music might be appropriate for God's people? There is. Three texts give us principles we can use. One is Philippians 4:8: "Finally, brethren, whatsoever things are true, whatsoever things are honest, whatsoever things are just, whatsoever things are pure, whatsoever things are lovely, whatsoever things are of good report; if there be any virtue, and if there be any praise, think on these things."

This text is more ambiguous than it seems at first. Does Paul counsel us to think only about things that meet all of these criteria? Is everything true lovely? Is everything lovely pure? How much praise is "any praise," and who is doing the praising? (Does "damning with faint praise" meet the requirement for "any praise"?)

How can we do this consistently while also doing our daily work? Does everything in the Bible meet these criteria? I think the answers are suggested in verse 9: "And the God of peace will be with you" (NIV). Paul is not making an explicit command here, but counseling us that if we think on these things, we will sense God's peace in us, and this will "guard your hearts and your minds in Christ Jesus" (verse 7, NIV). That is to say, thinking on these things helps us maintain our relationship with God, keeps us faithful.

Likewise, thinking about what is dishonest, unjust, impure,

ugly—thinking about what is sinful—draws us away from God. If we apply this principle to song lyrics, we can easily determine whether we should listen to them or sing them. If we want to be more like God, if we want to experience God's blessings, we should limit our exposure to things that don't draw us closer to Him. If you don't want to do that, what follows won't make much sense to you.

2) The second text that provides a useful principle is Colossians 3:16: "Let the word of Christ dwell in you richly in all wisdom; teaching and admonishing one another in psalms and hymns and spiritual songs, singing with grace in your hearts to the Lord" (KJV).

This is not specifically referring to a church service, but in verse 15 Paul refers to the Colossians as "members of one body" (NIV), which suggests a corporate application. Paul counsels the Colossians to fill themselves with the words of Christ (so seldom heard in churches today).

He asks them to use "psalms and hymns and spiritual songs" (the distinction between these three is still debated) for three purposes: to teach each other, to warn each other to be careful, and to sing to the Lord.[5] Furthermore, he asks that singing to the Lord be done "with grace in your hearts." I take this to refer to a sense of God's presence, perhaps an upwelling of love and gratefulness leading to emotional expression in song.

3) The third principle I find in the prayer of Jesus in John 17:20 and 21: "I pray also for those who will believe in me through their message, that all of them may be one, Father, just as you are in me and I am in you. May they also be in us so that the world may believe that you have sent me" (NIV).

Jesus was particularly concerned for the unity of His people. The divisions within Christendom make worldwide unity difficult, but

---

[5] Note that instrumental music does none of these. Teaching suggests song lyrics that help people understand doctrine or salvation. An example might be the hymn "The Church Has One Foundation." Admonition means mild reproof, and it might include encouragement. I think here of such hymns as "Soldiers of Christ, Arise" and "O Brother, Be Faithful." Singing to the Lord means songs of praise and worship or songs of petition, such as "Hear Our Prayer, O Lord."

even in the local congregation there are often divisions. When we allow them to continue, we keep Christ's prayer from being answered as He wished.

Whatever music we ourselves prefer, we must keep in mind the unity of God's people. Maintaining that unity may call for compromise, for accepting what we ourselves don't much like, for not insisting on our own musical preferences if some are offended by them.

Whatever combination of words and music meets these criteria is fine for praising God, whether or not I like it. That doesn't mean it's necessarily appropriate in the church building during the worship service, where there is a need for unity and there may be many people who don't like it, but it's appropriate for those who like it, whether they be alone or in a group with similar tastes.

Also, if any combination of words and music that meets these criteria proves itself able to touch the hearts of unbelievers, it can serve an evangelistic purpose, even though it might not be appropriate in an evangelistic campaign attended by a wide range of people.

From Principles to Imperatives

Principles are important. If we have sound principles on which to base our decisions, we can figure out what to do in any circumstance. The Bible also says more specific things about music, though, mostly in the Old Testament. In both Hebrew and English these comments are often written as imperatives. Imperatives are frequently commands, but sometimes they should be seen, rather, as good advice. At the least, though, if a biblical comment on music is stated as an imperative, we can be sure we will not be displeasing God if we do what it asks us to do.

These imperatives are generally written by poets. They are song lyrics. Some might say we shouldn't base our decisions on song lyrics, even if they are in the Scriptures, but this is not the usual Christian approach to the Bible. While we shouldn't think of these imperatives as commandments of God, never to be broken, we should at least take them seriously.

I've called this book *Joyful Noise* because the Bible urges us to "make a joyful noise" as we worship (Ps. 47; 66:1-4; 95:1-2; 98:4-9; 100). "Joyful noise," as used in the Psalms, does not mean polite murmuring during a song service. It does not mean singing without feeling because it's the right thing to do. It means singing enthusiastically, shouting hosannas and hallelujahs and amens because we feel them in our hearts. It's been a long time since I've heard that kind of noise in church.

Psalm 47:1 commands, "Clap your hands, all you peoples; shout to God with loud songs of joy" (NRSV). This is talking not about applause, but about clapping along with singing. Even if we grant that this is meant poetically or metaphorically and not as an absolute command, anyone who tries to prohibit rhythmic clapping as the church sings praises to God is going against what is clearly encouraged in Scripture.

Psalms 149 and 150 provide the names of a number of instruments we are to use in praising God: tambourines and cymbals (rhythm instruments), harps and lyres (guitar-like instruments), and flutes and trumpets (woodwind and brass instruments). Even if we don't accept the idea that these psalms actually command us to use these instruments, at the least we should admit that using them in worship must be pleasing to God.

Both psalms also urge us to "praise his name with dancing" (Ps. 149:3; 150:4). I'm not at all comfortable with praising God with dancing, and I have no interest in seeing dancing in churches, but I can't deny that it is biblical. I'm also far too shy to lift up my hands to God as I sing and pray, but this too is both condoned and commanded in the Scriptures (Ex. 9:29; Ps. 28:2; 63:4; 134:2; Isa. 1:15; Lam. 2:19; 1 Tim. 2:8).

Why do we condemn what God permits or commands? Why do we shy away from this counsel? Are we right to assume that God excuses or even approves of our shyness, our lack of enthusiasm, our love of tradition, silent meditation, and supposed reverence? Dare we claim that he despises those who do what the Scriptures allow or command?

Chapter 3

Guidelines for *Your* Music

Make a joyful noise to the Lord, all the earth;
break forth into joyous song and *sing praises.*
Sing praises to the Lord with the lyre,
with the lyre and the sound of melody.
With trumpets and the sound of the horn
make a joyful noise before the King, the Lord.
Let the sea *roar,* and all that fills it;
the world and those who live in it.
Let the floods *clap their hands;*
let the hills *sing together for joy*
at the presence of the Lord,
for he is coming to judge the earth.
He will judge the world with righteousness,
and the peoples with equity.
—Psalm 98:4-9, NRSV

In this chapter I'd like to suggest some guidelines Christians might use in choosing the music they listen to by themselves, whether for enjoyment or for personal worship of God. In the next chapter I'll suggest guidelines for music used in congregational worship.

The following suggestions are based on my belief that the most important thing in the world is establishing and maintaining a close, loving, and obedient relationship with God, what I call radical discipleship. This applies both on the personal level and in the church body.

If you want this kind of relationship, what follows will resonate in your heart. If you really aren't sure you want to submit yourself to God, what follows may make you angry, or it may seem like foolishness. But read on—you may find some good sense in all this, and you may even be persuaded.

We've looked at the scriptural principles we can easily apply in deciding what music deserves our attention. I've also found the following three criteria useful in judging not only music, but everything in life:

- ☙ What neither strengthens nor weakens a person's relationship with God may be tolerated within measure, but is suspect.
- ☙ Whatever weakens a person's relationship with God is dangerous and to be avoided.
- ☙ Whatever strengthens a person's relationship with God is praiseworthy, even if I myself don't happen to like it.

Some readers may consider these criteria dangerously permissive, opening the door to a variety of abuses. One critic told me this was the equivalent of saying, "If it feels good, it is good." That is definitely not my intention.

Jesus said, "But woe to you, scribes and Pharisees, hypocrites! For you lock people out of the kingdom of heaven. For you do not go in yourselves, and when others are going in, you stop them. . . . You tithe mint, dill, and cummin, and have neglected the weightier matters of the law: justice and mercy and faith. . . . You clean the outside of the cup and of the plate, but inside they are full of greed and self-indulgence" (Matt. 23:13, 23, 25, NRSV). Sometimes we commit ourselves so irrevocably to human traditions and personal tastes that we assume our way is the only way to God. When others reach God by some other way, we insist their route was false and their destination suspect. All roads to eternal life are narrow, but they are not identical. We each have our own crosses to bear.

The following suggestions are for those who agree with these criteria. Those who don't believe a relationship with God is important may not be convinced.

I also believe that this relationship with God is not a figure of speech. Instead, its presence is felt, sensed. When we find the "fruit of the Spirit" (Gal. 5:22) present in our lives, that is evidence of the relationship.

Enough warnings—read on.

1. No musical note or rhythm is morally right or wrong, good or bad. However, music affects the mind and the body in a variety of ways, and some combinations of notes, rhythms, tempos, and volume make it more difficult to walk with God. If the effect leads us away from God, the music should be avoided. If the effect does not lead us away from God, the music is acceptable, whatever its style.
Music can be judged good or bad on aesthetic grounds, but a badly composed piece of music is not morally sinful. Neither is a badly performed piece of music, even if it makes me flee the room. However, music played loudly enough to hear it properly has a physiological effect on people, and this physiological effect can in turn cause a psychological effect. Some musical performances have physiological or psychological effects that encourage sinful actions or thoughts. People who want to walk with God should avoid this music. Judge the music by its fruits. Be honest—don't let your personal tastes interfere with your judgment. You may have to give up something you love or accept something you don't like.

Some music speeds up the heart rate and makes one want to march, tap one's feet, wave one's hand as if conducting, beat out a rhythm on the nearest available object, or even dance. This music may help one do repetitive tasks quickly. It can also make one feel happy. This is not a question of moral goodness or badness in the music, but a simple cause-and-effect relationship, with the beat, tempo, and volume of the music leading to physiological change, leading in turn to psychological change. To feel energetic and happy is not sinful or bad.

Other music calms the heart and stills the mind. This music may help one relax after a difficult day or accomplish a complex task one isn't eager to do, such as writing a college paper or balancing the checkbook. This is also neither morally good nor bad in itself. Just as it is not sinful to feel energetic or happy, it is not sinful to feel calm and peaceful. Some have suggested that a lowered heart rate is always a good thing, but a heart rate increased a few beats per minute by music is seldom a health problem, especially for young people.

Almost any style of music can be used to convey a Christian message, though some are more effective at sharing God than others. There are some styles, however, that even without words are dark and menacing. Listeners feel increasingly depressed and desperate. There is music that makes people feel paranoid, angry, or lustful. While the notes and rhythms are not morally evil, any more than letters are evil because they can be formed into words that cause harm, the feelings these notes and rhythms generate contradict the spirit of Christianity. Desperation, depression, and paranoia do not come from God. Jesus prohibits anger and lust. I would suggest that Christians shouldn't listen to this music, because these feelings are at odds with the good news of salvation.[1] Any music that has evil effects should be shunned. For example, Beethoven's Fifth Symphony is an aesthetic triumph. I admire it very much on an artistic level. Nevertheless, the music fills me with foreboding, despair, and anger, so I choose not to listen to it.

This is the heart of this book's message. For decades authors have lumped together all rock music (or pop or jazz or rap or whatever) as if it were all the same and so should all have the same effect. These authors have looked for extreme examples that disgust most people. Then, pointing to these extremes, they've argued that all varieties of whatever form of music is being demonized are dangerous. Because this argument is only partially true, it is a false argument, and young people are smart enough to know that. They respond by rejecting the entire argument.

Let's play fair. Let's agree that some feelings tempt people to sin in some way and that God's people should avoid these feelings. Let's agree that some combinations of notes and rhythms and volume give

---

[1] There are rare exceptions—such as the "Dies Irae" section of Verdi's *Requiem*. The music is dark and violent, yet acceptable for Christians—in this case because it portrays the wrath of God against sin on the day of judgment.

people these feelings. Let's put all types of music on the table—not only rock music and pop music in their many varieties, but all the various subcategories of classical music, opera, folk music, ethnic music of all sorts, everything, all of the several hundred types. Let's agree that whether or not the music has lyrics and whether or not they are ostensibly Christian lyrics, we will try to avoid any music that gives us these feelings that can lead us to sin.

Judging a tree by its fruit, not its leaves, is a sound biblical principle (while Matthew 7:16-20 is talking about discovering false prophets, the principle behind Jesus' statement is correctly applied to other types of judging, as well). Imagine, for example, the many kinds of rock music as varieties of apples in an orchard. There are many varieties of apples. Some are old-fashioned "heirloom" varieties, perhaps unusual and tasty, but perhaps rightfully nearly extinct. Some popular varieties are nearly tasteless, but chosen for looks and easy shipping. Many of the most delicious varieties are seldom found in markets. Some varieties of apples, however, aren't good for anything. They don't taste very good, their texture is mealy, they are misshapen, and they are prone to disease. They aren't good for fresh eating, pies, applesauce, or cider. After we've tasted the fruit and made sure it can't be improved by cultivating or fertilizing (Luke 13:6-8; Matt. 12:33), we should cut the tree down and burn it. What we shouldn't do is cut down our entire orchard, with its many varieties of apples, merely because a few varieties aren't worth keeping.

If we imagine classical music as varieties of pears in the same orchard, we may notice that many varieties are sweet and juicy, some are better hard, some are more fragrant than others, and some are grainy and others smooth-fleshed. Some are wonderful fresh, while others are valuable because they preserve their flavor and texture when canned. We need to admit that as with apples, some varieties aren't worth growing. We shouldn't argue that because it's a pear, it must be good. Likewise, we shouldn't condemn all apples because they are not pear-shaped or don't taste like pears. That's what many critics of popular music have done.

Let's be sensible. Inspecting fruit is not difficult: we need only taste and see. Let's use our God-given gift of discernment and be more discriminating. Let's root out trees producing bad fruit wherever we find them, but let's not cut and burn trees producing good fruit, merely because we don't like that type of fruit. (I'm the only person in my family who likes gooseberries and red currants. I would be very annoyed if I came home to find that my children had pulled up all of my gooseberry and red currant bushes because they don't like them.)

I believe young people will respond to this sensible approach. They will respect us for adopting it. Adopting it will decrease the tension between generations. Whether we like it or not, there are a great many young people who want to be like Jesus, yet listen to secular popular music all the time, not realizing how this is interfering with their walk with God. If we adopt this more sensible, less prejudiced view, I think many young people will follow our lead, judging more carefully and giving up what they see is harming them.

I don't think composers should try to connect music that leads to sinful feelings with a Christian message. If they are Christians, they should be mature enough to notice the disparity between the music and the message and turn instead to some other form of music. There are plenty to choose from. (Oddly, while this problematic music is generally found only in a tiny segment of rock music, we need to admit that there are also styles of "serious music" that have this effect. Some argue that this music is merely reflecting the anxiety of our times. This may well be, but Christians don't need that anxiety in their lives.)

We don't know what music David played for Saul when Saul suffered mental and emotional distress, but people have long known that music can change moods and make people feel better. Just as it is good to eat food that makes us physically healthy, it is good to listen to music that helps us be emotionally healthy. Again, judge it by its fruits. If the fruit is nasty, cut down the tree. If one style of music proves to be unhealthy, there are certainly many healthy styles you can learn to enjoy.

Today researchers know that vigorous singing or similar physical participation in music can release naturally occurring chemicals in the brain that ease pain or lead to a feeling of well-being. Such feelings are not in themselves spiritual, but when they accompany the spiritual they intensify it and encourage unity, joy, and care for others.

2. Christians should be very cautious about "secular music." A large percentage of the lyrics of such songs, no matter what the style, don't meet the standards outlined in Philippians 4:8. It's not easy for Christians to keep their minds fixed on heavenly things. Any Christian music helps those who like it, but the lyrics of secular music generally don't.

This caution applies to the lyrics of any kind of secular music. Broadway show tunes, operatic arias, Celtic ballads, classical lieder, and country-western songs are as likely to be problematic as rock music.

If we want to walk with God as consistently and fruitfully as possible, we should simply not listen to music with lyrics that make us consider doing things Christians shouldn't do. This needn't be seen as a great sacrifice. The good effects outweigh what we give up. Also, just as for those who like meat but want to be vegetarians there are meat substitutes, there are Christian substitutes for all of these types of music. (Like meat substitutes, they may be less tasty than the real thing, and they may take some getting used to, but they are much better for you.)

I've often heard young people say, "I don't listen to the lyrics, so they don't harm me. I just like the music." If that's the case, however, why, when pressed, do they turn out to know the lyrics to great numbers of songs on the radio?

The problem with these lyrics isn't really that, say, listening to someone croon about the pleasures of illicit sex makes one want to go and do likewise (though it might). Listening to a song about killing cops doesn't make most people want to kill cops.

However, illicit sex and killing cops are not pure, virtuous, or praiseworthy. Songs about these acts will thus interfere with our experience of purity, virtue, and praiseworthiness, because they get into our minds and are difficult to get out.

Some lyrics don't seem "all that bad." For example, many pop songs are about love. What's wrong with love? What's wrong with a song in which a boy sings "I'll love you forever" to his girlfriend?

Songs like this encourage romantic notions at tender ages and teach unrealistic ideas about love. If one hears them too often, one gets the idea that this kind of romance is a bigger part of life than it really is. Romance, like dessert, is good, but best in moderation. (Can listening to a great deal of CCM lead people to think that God should be a major part of their lives? Yes, of course! That's part of its purpose!)

Hearing these songs now and then in the shopping mall is not a major problem, but because they may not be true and virtuous, they get in the way of our walk with God. It really isn't all that easy to maintain a walk with God day after day. Anything that can help is worth a try. Anything that doesn't help should be reconsidered.

Some lyrics deal with human things rather than godly things, but are not impure. For example, some songs are about nature. Others are protests against oppression, reminding us of things that are unpleasant but true.[2] Some songs are comic, and others tell stories. This music does little harm in moderation, apart from sometimes taking time that could be devoted to better things. Of course, it won't do to listen for these songs on the radio, because one doesn't know when they will come on.

Recently my sons and I have been pondering what to do about

_____

[2] In the years before Bob Dylan and I gave our lives to God, his album *Street Legal* (1978, a year before his first Christian album), which I listened to over and over, kept raising a longing for God in my life. Whether or not he knew it at the time, his songs were crying out for salvation. ("Will I be able to count on you?" he asks in "Is Your Love in Vain?" In "Señor" he sings, "I'm ready when you are, señor," then suggests that they overturn the tables, echoing Christ's actions in the temple, because "This place don't make sense to me no more.") I heard these songs as prayers, as cries from a struggling heart (I knew that "Señor" in Spanish means not only "mister" but "Lord"). Last summer I listened to them again, after not hearing them for years, and I was moved to tears as I sensed the Holy Spirit chasing Dylan like Francis Thompson's Hound of Heaven.

CDs by the bands P.O.D. and MxPx that they purchased at a Christian bookstore. We've been listening together to these CDs. The problem isn't that these are punk rock bands, because there are punk rock bands that have a good spiritual message. The problem is that we can't make out many of the words, and the words we can figure out don't seem especially spiritual. I'm not at all sure there is a significant difference between listening to a Christian band with undecipherable lyrics and listening to a secular band with undecipherable lyrics. Neither one helps listeners draw closer to God.

I'm willing to stand up for any song, no matter what its style, that really does help people focus on God, but not for songs that don't have that effect. It may seem odd, but sometimes a Christian band's witness is negated when the record producer turns down the vocals when doing the sound mix. Inaudible vocals may be stylish in some sorts of music, but here's a place where Christians need to buck the style. Christian music, whatever the style, is most effective when the vocals are in the foreground. (I'm praying that my sons will decide they don't want to listen to these CDs with inaudible vocals anymore.)

3. Music videos and MTV are nearly always more problematic for the Christian than the songs alone. They demand more attention than the songs alone, they glorify the performers beyond their musicianship, they often introduce themes of sex or violence not present in the songs themselves, and because they are often lip-synched, they seem insincere. The primary exception is some videos of concerts. Even Christian music videos move the focus from the song to the performer, degrading the spiritual message.

If the purpose of CCM is to turn the hearts of listeners to God, as claimed, we do well to notice that Christian music videos turn the attention to the performer.

There is a natural interest in seeing what performers look like and how they play. This is part of why people go to concerts rather than merely listening to CDs—no matter what the style of music. This in itself isn't a problem, because the concert doesn't last long. (The performers share the limelight with God for an hour, then retreat into the background.) Similarly, watching a video of a concert isn't much of a problem.

When a song is turned into an MTV-style music video, however, a scriptwriter and director take over—often not themselves Christians—and they may change a song's focus as they use their unsanctified imaginations to make a song more entertaining.

This means not that young people shouldn't watch Christian music videos, but that they should be cautious and not make them part of their daily diet.

However, Christians would do well not to watch non-Christian music videos at all. Such a large proportion of the videos on MTV are impure in some way that one might as well be watching the "hot" scenes from R-rated movies.[3]

The popularity of MTV with many young people suggests that watching music videos can become almost compulsive behavior. Experience and reason quickly reveal that it is very difficult to maintain one's focus on God while watching these videos.[4]

Many music videos cost as much to make as advertisements and much more, minute for minute, than most movies. The reason is

---

[3] A few weeks ago I walked into Best Buys to purchase an ink cartridge for my printer and was accosted by a 20-foot wide bank of television screens hooked up to work as one huge screen. On the screens was a music video of pop singer Britney Spears. Her nearly naked torso could be seen from across the store. As she lip-synched her song she caressed her flesh and offered each body part to the camera as to a lover. When I was close enough to hear the words, I was surprised to find that she was singing a relatively inoffensive love song. The video portion of the performance said something quite different from the lyrics, however. An hour spent watching music videos on MTV will reveal many similar examples.

[4] Let's be fair. It's also hard to maintain one's focus on God while watching the evening news or sports or just about any television program. There is very little in the news that is pure, lovely, or indeed entirely true—television news is a wallow in filth garbed in the supposedly hallowed robes of relevance and importance, interspersed with frequent appeals to sensual gratification and worship of worldliness (called advertising). By contrast, some Christian television can help us keep our eyes on God, much as CCM does—though some is sensationalistic or theologically suspect, and the frequent requests for donations are appalling (see Acts 8:18-24).

that video directors try to make them as compelling as possible, hoping to keep viewers watching. Unfortunately, sex and violence draw our attention, so they are emphasized in videos.

4. Each style of music has its own criteria for excellence of composition and performance. We can't fairly judge one style by the criteria for another style. Other things being equal, excellence is preferable to mediocrity, because excellence comes closer to the creative perfection of God.

We don't complain that the leopard is inadequate because it doesn't have stripes like a tiger. We don't think less of the chicken because it doesn't bark like a dog. Similarly, we need to judge Christian music, whatever its style, according to the conventions of that style.

Some university-trained professional musicians believe the only appropriate music for worship is "serious music," and that the highly trained operatic voice is most suitable for the gospel (despite the fact that it is sometimes difficult to understand the words).[5] This is simply not true.

As I write, the Winter Olympic Games at Salt Lake City have just ended. What if the judges in the figure skating competitions marked skaters down because of insufficient speed? What if the judges in the speed skating competitions marked down speed skaters because they didn't leap into the air and spin? Yet within each competition excellence can be judged (though, as with music, there is a necessary subjectivity to this judging).

Similarly, we can easily determine whether classical music is well performed, but if we judge it according to the conventions of bluegrass, the best of it will fall far short. That doesn't mean bluegrass

---

[5] For example, Calvin M. Johansson's chapters in *The Christian & Rock Music*. See my review in chapter 6 for a refutation of his elitist ideas about music and worship. Some operatic singers, such as my friend Chuck Reid, trained at Westminster Choir College in Princeton, New Jersey, specialize in singing not only beautifully but intelligibly. Reid's specialty is sacred oratories, and he believes it is crucial that the words be understood.

music is better than classical. It simply means it's a different style.

If we judge Christian rock according to whether it is as melodically and harmonically complex as some classical music, it will of course fall short, but that isn't what it intends to do, nor are the criteria of classical music divinely revealed.

There is a substantial joy to be gained from what is melodically and harmonically simple, as well as from what is complex. Many of us who play instruments can play only what is simple, and if only what is complex is praiseworthy, then we won't be able to play. Yet even what is simple can praise God.

In singing as well, the criteria for excellence vary with the style. In country-western vocals a southern accent is expected, and a little sob or yodel in the voice is appreciated. In bluegrass a bit more twang in the voice is appropriate. White blues singers are expected to sing with Black accents.

In opera, the voice is more an instrument of beauty than communication. On the other hand, in Broadway musicals singers are supposed to have interesting voices rather than beautiful ones.

Today's rhythm and blues singers have developed their own ways of replacing held notes with little arpeggios, turning one note into five or six. Black gospel uses some similar techniques in singing, but White gospel needs a plainer voice, preferably with some sort of Appalachian whine.

Jazz singers have to croon with beautiful voices, but their sense of rhythm is far different from that of opera singers. An operatic voice may at its best be the acme of human vocal achievement, but it sounds ludicrous, wildly inappropriate, with rock music. It can also sound out of place with praise songs.

Each of these vocal types can be very pleasant to listen to. Each can appropriately communicate the Christian message. We can't fairly denigrate one appropriate style of singing because it isn't another appropriate style of singing.

However, within a single style of music, we can fairly judge the relative merits of voices. Some have a more pleasing sound, greater range, more accurate intonation. We can fairly prefer excellence to mediocrity, and we can train performers.

Nevertheless, we need to bear in mind that there are many singers who have a gift for conveying spiritual things in music, even though their voices are nothing special.

I'm not saying that it's as difficult to sing folk music as it is to sing opera, or that some country blues tune is equal in compositional complexity and excellence to a Brahms symphony. I am saying that each has its own criteria for quality, even if some styles require more training than others. God can be praised in every style.

What's more, the God who loves and heals sinners and prefers the poor in spirit to the proud must certainly take at least as much delight in hearing the screechiest 6-year-old violinist, who loves him with all their heart, as in hearing the pure notes of the professional who receives a check and shows up only when performing (though I'd rather listen to the professional). There is room for all creatures of our God and King to praise Him.

5. Spiritual, emotional, and intellectual sincerity and authenticity are valid criteria for judging music and lyrics. Quality of composition and performance in any style of music cannot make up for lack of evident sincerity. In worship, excellence without sincerity borders on blasphemy.

It's been said, "You've got to suffer if you want to sing the blues,"[6] and this has an application to other styles of music too. We should, perhaps, be disturbed to hear people sing "Redeemed! how I love to proclaim it!" when they haven't been born again and don't love to proclaim their relationship with God.

---

[6] This is one reason the Negro spiritual is not usually the best choice for a choir of white college students. They may enjoy the song, but in their mouths it loses the integrity it once had, because the dialect is not their own. Those interested in the background of this type of music should read Thomas Wentworth Higginson's groundbreaking article "Negro Spirituals," published in the June 1867 issue of the *Atlantic Monthly,* but available online at several sites, such as http://xroads.Virginia.edu/~HYPER/TWH/Higg.html.

Jesus was more pleased by the widow who gave her last two mites than with the trumpeted charity of the rich. I think He would be more pleased by the creaky-voiced grandmother who breaks down in tears while singing "Jesus Paid It All" than by the opera singer who can sing "Agnus Dei" in a piercingly beautiful voice but has never surrendered herself to the Lamb of God.

Even those who walk with God can't sing all songs with sincerity. A song about being lifted up from the gutter is not convincing from the mouth of someone who has never turned away from God.

Canned music is inherently lacking in sincerity, so singing to a taped accompaniment during the worship service is not generally the best way to bring people to God (I've heard it called "sacred karaoke").

Some Christian songs strike me as less heartfelt than others. Some seem less than authentic and more like attempts to make money or tug on emotional heartstrings (sentimentalism).

As a child of the late sixties and early seventies, times when authenticity and sincerity were considered important virtues, I have a special respect for performers who write their own songs, even if their voices and playing are less than superb. I don't mean to say that performers should write their own songs for worship, but I do think believability should be on the list of criteria when we judge a performance.

6. Some Christian lyrics contain theological errors. This is not a large problem for the spiritually mature, but it can confuse those who are not biblically literate. Thus we should consider whether the pleasure we gain from a song outweighs the potential harm of biblically inaccurate lyrics.

Few Christian songwriters are theologians. Most of them reflect what they've read, what music they've heard, and what their pastors say. Thus it's not surprising that some songs have lyrics that reveal a misunderstanding of the Bible.

This is perhaps least likely with praise songs drawn straight from the Bible and with the great eighteenth century hymns written by poets who were theologically sophisticated.[7] It is more of a problem with Negro spirituals and Black and White southern gospel. I'm very fond of many of these songs, and I don't mean that we shouldn't use them, especially since they can be very effective at bringing unity to a group of believers. I am saying simply that some really have very little scriptural support, and we might do better to prefer the sounder ones.

"Swing Low, Sweet Chariot" is a delightful song, fun to sing if it swings a little, but those who don't realize how it draws on the Elijah story and uses symbols to represent actual events might come to expect Christ to carry them away in a chariot.

The gospel favorites "I'll Fly Away" and "Great Speckled Bird" are also less than biblically accurate. I've heard "Ave Maria" sung in Protestant worship services several times, but while I love the melody, I disagree with the sentiment expressed.

While I myself much prefer the great old hymns, I would strongly urge those who agree with me to bear in mind that our most important duty is to bring people to Christ rather than turn them away from Him.

We have a special duty to bring our children to God, rather than alienate them. We should be willing to sacrifice our own tastes in order to keep our children with us, and we should make certain that what we assume to be our principles are not in fact merely our tastes.

In the next chapter we will look at music in congregational worship. Apart from corporate worship, however, if the music causes no harmful effects and if the lyrics are pure, virtuous, praiseworthy, and especially if they help the individual walk with God, I think God approves and blesses, no matter what the style of music. Parents who take this approach—whatever their own tastes—will be less likely to alienate their children.

---

[7] Though indeed these hymns are often rewritten or have problematic verses left out.

Chapter 4

Guidelines for *Our* Music: Congregational Worship

Make *a joyful noise* to the Lord, all the earth.
Worship the Lord with *gladness;*
come into his presence with *singing.*
Know that the Lord is God.
It is he that made us, and we are his;
we are his people, and the sheep of his pasture.
Enter his gates with *thanksgiving,*
and his courts with *praise.*
Give thanks to him, *bless his name.*
For the Lord is good;
his steadfast love endures forever,
and his faithfulness to all generations.
—Psalm 100, NRSV

   True worship, whether individual or corporate, is different from the "going through the motions" so common in churches today. It fills us with joy, with love, with peace. It makes us feel kinship with other believers. Sometimes this may remind us of Wordsworth's silent and solitary nun, "breathless with adoration." At other times it may lead to ecstatic praise or choruses of amens. Not everyone feels it all the time or with a similar intensity, but when we feel it, we sense God's presence.

  Whether silent or noisy, a church service without this sense of God's presence may be a church service without true worship. If we truly understand what God has done for us, how can we remain dry-eyed? My suggestions in this chapter aim at producing and maintaining the sense of God's presence in the believer and the worship service.

I'm not advocating a feelings-based worship service that abandons reason and sound teaching, but if we feel nothing during the worship service, how do we know God is with us? The Bible teaches us to verify our faith by looking for experiential evidence that it is alive. If we leave the worship service unmoved and without seeing any sign that others in the congregation were moved, we should wonder whether we have really worshiped.

I'm also not suggesting that all churches adopt the "celebration worship" style that frightens some church members. It's possible to make a lot of noise during worship without being deeply moved and called to repentance by the Holy Spirit. However, neither am I condemning it. This type of service is often the most effective way of helping people enter into God's presence. I'm also not advocating worship services that are primarily entertainment, rather than participation. People can be brought to God through entertainment, but participation is more effective.

Finally, I am not saying that people cannot experience God's presence in a traditional service. There are quite a few traditional worship services in which one senses true love for one another, true surrender, true worship. Some of them are large, some small. Some are loud, some quiet. I've experienced God's presence most frequently in African-American and Hispanic congregations, but I've also found it elsewhere on occasion. If the members of a congregation find that traditional elements bring them to God, they needn't change. However, it's worthwhile to examine our form of worship carefully and see if it is as effective for the whole congregation as it is for us.

Let's look again at the three statements made in the previous chapter that I find useful in judging not only music, but everything in life:

☙ What neither strengthens nor weakens a person's relationship with God may be tolerated within measure, but is suspect.

☙ Whatever weakens a person's relationship with God is dangerous and to be avoided.

✍ Whatever strengthens a person's relationship with God is praiseworthy, even if I myself don't happen to like it.

Now, let's look at music for congregational worship.

1. Music is not of itself sacred or secular, whatever its style. Classical and sacred are not synonymous. Quality of composition or performance does not make music without words suitable for the worship service. When instrumental music calls to mind sacred lyrics, it can lead to worship, though generally less efficiently than music with words. At best, from a spiritual viewpoint, music without words in the worship service provides a background for meditation. However, many listeners don't make use of this opportunity.

Some people assume that any classical music is appropriate in the worship service because it has no words and its beauty and excellence praise God. However, while such music may be so beautiful that it makes us thank God, we are more likely to enjoy it simply because it is beautiful, with no conscious thought of God.

It may be edifying to the intellect and the emotions, but it is not generally spiritually edifying to most listeners. At best it provides a pleasant background to the Spirit's working on the heart during meditation, should we choose to meditate. More often it holds our attention and keeps us from such meditation.

There are times instrumental music might provide a background for whatever else is going on, such as before the worship service begins or after it ends. However, if it calls to mind spiritual lyrics familiar to most people in the audience, it will have more spiritual impact.

Thus playing hymns on the organ may do more to bring the congregation to God than playing a Bach fugue, even though the fugue was dedicated to God's glory and exhibits a greater technical excellence.

Our primary concern as we consider what music to use in the worship service should be its effect on the worshipers. Does it bring them to a unity of spirit? Does it make them more receptive to the work of the Holy Spirit? Does it help convince them of their need of a Savior, remind them there's power in the blood, encourage them to be like Jesus, inspire them to praise God with their whole heart?

Meditative organ music may prepare some people to receive the Holy Spirit quietly, but it does little to make a group of people feel "of one accord," and there are more effective ways of ushering in the Spirit, such as singing hymns with heartfelt sincerity.

Outside the worship service, instrumental music is less of a problem. Listening to classical music is an aesthetically positive but spiritually neutral occupation, in general, though it has physiological and psychological effects that have a bearing on our spiritual focus.

Some "serious music" is disturbing, but most isn't. It can make a pleasant background for daily life. However, songs with Christian lyrics, performed in a style we appreciate, do much more to keep us close to God, whatever their level of excellence.

2. Any style of music can entertain. Entertainment is not in itself wrong, in its place, but the worship service is not the best place for entertainment, because the more we are being entertained, the less we are worshiping. Thus the worship service will be more spiritually profitable if we avoid music that entertains. "Special music" in the worship service can sometimes provide an opportunity for meditation or allow God to speak to the listener, but primarily, I believe, it entertains the congregation, despite the performers' desire to give glory to God.

Some condemn certain kinds of CCM because they are entertaining, but any time performers perform and people watch rather than participating, the watchers are being entertained, even when that music is "serious." The performer may be praising God, and some of those listening may be praising God as a result of the performance, but the fact remains that the primary purpose of "special music" is providing a special treat for the listeners, which is to say, entertainment.

My friend Chuck Reid, an opera and oratorio soloist, has objected that any music we find enjoyable entertains us, even if we are singing congregational hymns. He is right, but I am using the word in a different sense. By music that entertains, I mean music performed to give the audience pleasure, music performed while the audience listens, rather than music that includes and involves the audience. Some critics have blasted certain styles of music as entertainment, assuming that "serious music" performed in church is not entertaining. I don't think this argument is sound. True, some audiences do not find "serious music" very entertaining, but whatever the style of music, when people perform for an audience, their intent is entertaining the audience, even if they claim to be performing for God.

We expect to be entertained if we attend a concert, and this sort of Christian entertainment can be a good thing. Some people experience God in a powerful way during such entertainment. We are being entertained when we listen to music at home, yet God can still talk to us. The primary problem with entertainment during the church service is that while some people may be brought to God by it, it isn't the most effective way to bring the entire congregation to a sense of unity at once. Achieving that unity is so important that we should be willing to set aside our traditional "spectator" approach to worship. (It's true that during some concerts the entire audience feels a sense of corporate unity—Grateful Dead concerts were famous for this. During some Christian concerts the whole audience worships together and senses God's Spirit among them. However, this effect is generally accompanied by sound levels unacceptable in many church services.)

True worship is not a spectator sport. Watching someone else worship is not in itself worship.

Of course, it's possible to worship while watching or listening. It's simply not the *most effective* way of achieving unity in worship. I recently took my sons, ages 11 and 13 at the time, to their first CCM concert, one they very much wanted to see: Jennifer Knapp and her band and Jars of Clay. These are among the most talented CCM composers and performers. In concert, however, the music was deafening, the sound systems rather crude, and I rarely understood a word the vocalists sang, though my sons were enthralled. I was impressed by the clean-cut modesty of the some five thousand young people present and the lack of smoke, alcohol, and drugs (very much present at concerts in my rock 'n' roll days).

What most impressed me, however, was looking around at those sitting or standing nearby. As the music roared about us, hundreds of these teenagers and college students had their eyes closed and their faces and hands lifted up to God. They knew every word, and they were singing along with the bands, but where the bands were entertaining, these young people were worshiping. Indeed, I might even say they were completely immersed in worship and communion with God. Frankly, I was jealous. If I saw more of that during special music or organ preludes when the church gathers to worship, my comments would be less pejorative.

In 1 Corinthians 14:26, Paul tells us something about how worship sometimes occurred in New Testament times. He writes, "What should be done then, my friends? When you come together, each one has a hymn, a lesson, a revelation, a tongue, or an interpretation" (NRSV).

This verse is less clear than it seems, but I take it to mean that in Corinth (a church with every problem in the book, though also with good qualities), everyone liked to have a part in the worship service. I suspect that ideally they would take turns rising and sharing. It was a sort of spiritual amateur hour.

Paul doesn't condemn this, and it shouldn't be seen as entertainment, though it could degenerate into prideful performance if not controlled. I see it more as a sort of testimony service, with everyone edified by hearing what God was doing in the lives of their brothers and sisters.

Paul then provides the principle on which to rate these things: "Let all things be done for building up" (verse 26, NRSV). I think that means we should evaluate everything in our worship service by whether or not it helps people draw closer to God and stay closer to God.

I place "special music" in quotes because often it's not very special, and if it is scheduled every week it's doubly not special. I think I would feel better about it if the singer sang from the congregation rather than from the platform, so there would be less emphasis on the performer.

(Ironically, my wife recently scheduled herself, our son Peter, our daughter Mary, and me to provide "special music" at our church—my wife on viola, Peter on bass, Mary on tenor recorder, and me on guitar. This was our first such performance, and I assure you "special" was not the best word for it. However, we minimized the damage by inviting the congregation to sing along. Playing together at home is fun, but I'm not sure we're ready for "prime time.")

The hand-held microphones and seemingly calculated poses and gestures I often see during "special music" seem more like entertainment than worship. Perhaps performers would do well to ask themselves, "Is this my individual worship, regardless of anyone else who may be listening? Am I trying to lift the other worshipers to God by sharing with them a song that will edify them, or am I really trying to please them, entertain them, or elicit their praise?"

When one listens to music in the car or the home, entertainment is not out of place, but there are various types of entertainment. Being entertained by music in private even as one is lifted to God by it is quite acceptable. As I've explained above, music videos have so much entertainment that the edification can be missed, but this problem needn't happen with music one hears. Some times with God are better than other times with God, but any time with God is better than no time with God.

Some will ask, at this point, "What about applause during the worship service?" I know the argument that we aren't applauding the performer, but the message, or God, but the fact is that we don't applaud God after we sing a congregational hymn. Thus whatever we may pretend, applause after "special music" is nearly always performer-focused, and thus questionable. I don't get applause after I preach a terrific sermon (admittedly a rare occurrence), so why should we applaud a musician during the worship service?

Actually, we applaud during the worship service because we are used to applauding at secular performances, but in so doing we make it clear that "special music" is more entertainment than worship. I have no problem with applauding a Christian entertainer performing at a concert, even if that concert is in the room where the church meets to worship, because a Christian concert may praise God and may lead people to Him, but it is not communal worship. Concerts often bring people into unity, but their purpose is not congregational unity as an essential element of corporate worship.

However, I think applause during the worship service is a sign that we need to rethink whether worship should entertain us or be something we do together. (Similarly, I cringe at the trend these days for pastors to say, "Let's give God a big hand of applause." If God has done some mighty act, we'd do much better to begin singing the Doxology spontaneously.)

Experience shows us that God doesn't strike us dead or send fire from heaven to destroy us if we applaud during the worship service. If I were a pastor, I don't think eliminating such applause would be high on my agenda, because the church will not begin worshiping "in spirit and in truth" (John 4:24) merely because it no longer applauds performers. This would be about as effective as a plastic surgeon bestowing youth and beauty by doing a nose job on an 80-year-old person who weighs 400 pounds. The body of Christ needs a much more substantial makeover before true worship will happen every time it meets.

Clapping the hands rhythmically during congregational singing is quite a different matter. Psalm 47:1 urges us, "Clap your hands, all you peoples; shout to God with loud songs of joy" (NRSV). True, some hymns and praise songs don't lend themselves well to clapping, but if they do, it seems that this joyful clapping during loud singing pleases God.

3. Everything in the worship service should encourage an intense unity of the believers, a unity of thought, feeling, and worship, preparing believers to receive God's Word to them. Any element of the service that lowers congregational fervor or detracts from congregational unity should be changed or deleted. Silence should not be equated with true reverence or worship (though true worship is often silent, of course).

I admit that this is an unusual position. However, what most concerned Jesus as He prayed in John 17 was the unity of the believers. Three times Jesus commanded, "Love one another" (John 13:34; 15:12, 17). I assume he meant it.

It seems to me that we praise and worship God best when we do it from a position of loving unity. When we are filled with love for each other, when we come to feel open to each other, concerned about each other, connected to each other, then I think we can feel the Holy Spirit descend upon us, whether we be silent or singing, and true worship begins.

I have sat in hundreds of worship services where I've felt that little worship was occurring because there was no connection between those present. I've sat in services in the same rooms that were foretastes of heaven, with God's presence very near.

In my own life, I experience this most often at camp meeting. The evening meetings are often held in the same room where I worship every week, but the people are different. Those who come to spend a whole week at camp meeting are eager to receive a blessing, they are confident that it will happen, and it does. (What a treat to speak to groups like this.) Too often, those who sit there once a week are there because it's the right or required thing to do. This isn't really worship.

It's harder to reach this unity in a large church than in a small church, and it's harder to reach it in a nearly empty church than in a full church.

The unity can sometimes be faked if people sing loud enough, but there is a true unity that transcends volume. Unity is very diffi-cult to achieve when a congregation sits in pews looking at the back of the heads of the people in front of them.

Unity can be more easily achieved by merely angling the pews, so it's easier to turn one's head and see and hear the other wor-shipers. Then one feels less alone. Better yet is people sitting in a cir-cle, and even better, people sitting at home in a living room, praising God together.

I believe that everything in the worship service needs to be sub-ordinate to the goal of worshiping God in unity. If the organ pre-lude and the special music lower the spiritual temperature by drawing people away from each other and focusing on a private ex-perience of God, replace them with congregational hymns.

If taking up the offering distracts people from God, collect it ear-lier or later.

If the verse or two that far too often passes for a scripture read-ing and the "morning prayer" don't inflame the congregation, then replace them with a season of prayer and Bible quoting and singing that lasts an hour, rippling back and forth across the congregation and gathering the worshipers together as a harvester gathers wheat into sheaves.

Then, when the church is one as the Father and the Son are *one* (John 17:11), when the church has joyfully and tearfully praised God as one and lifted up each other to God, let God the gracious King respond to His people, guiding them and training them, admonish-ing and comforting, through the person of His ambassador, the pas-tor. I long for this. I believe God longs for this.

Some might say I am mistaking manufactured emotions for gen-uine worship, or that I am trying to conjure up the Spirit. I don't think so.

Consider the difference between watching your favorite football game while sitting in the stadium and watching it at home with the television's sound turned down low. You can see better at home, but you entirely miss the physiological and psychological transformation that comes from being with 50,000 people who are loudly of one accord.

Imagine what would happen if you invited a dozen people to your home, then made them sit in rows in your living room, with no eye contact. Would that increase the feeling of caring friendship?

Recall the difference between visiting with a dear friend face to face and visiting by telephone. I remember, a generation ago, talking on a pay phone in England to my fiancée in California once a week for 10 minutes (all I could afford). The experience was more frustrating than fulfilling.

What passes for worship often seems like that to me.[1] It can be both disconcerting and disheartening to look at people in the church service and see profound boredom on their faces.

Perhaps I simply have a harder time letting go of myself than do most people, but I believe there is a large core of thoughtful people who are deeply unhappy with the worship service, who are starving for a sense of holy community, of being "one in the Spirit," as the song claims, of not only being acquainted with each other but of loving each other. If to obey is truly better than sacrifice, we should obey our Lord and love one another.

Music, used rightly, is one of the most effective ways of reaching this state. If young people were accustomed to reaching it every week by singing the great old hymns, they would be less interested in trying other musical styles that might help them reach it.

I think we should choose music for the worship service according to its effectiveness in moving us to this blessed state. I don't think instrumental music does this effectively.

It can be done with hymns, with praise songs, with Black gospel

---

[1] Not always, though. Last week the room was packed, the hymns sung with vigor, and we sang one of my favorites, "For All the Saints." I couldn't sing the last verse. I was too choked up and overwhelmed by the ocean roar of voices describing what I most long for: "From earth's wide bounds, from ocean's farthest coast, / Thro' gates of pearl streams in the countless host, / Singing to Father, Son, and Holy Ghost, / Alleluia, Alleluia!" That's worship! That's what I'm pleading for!

and White gospel, even with the accompaniment of a rock band, so long as the worshipers aren't offended by the music.

A congregation that doesn't know or like the old hymns I love might want to try something else (though there is much to be said for training people during afternoon hymn sings).[2] A congregation that gags at drums and electric guitars can usually compromise on other types of music. I suspect, though, that if the congregation is really intent on entering into worship, any of these styles of music will work.

4. Congregational singing is the only music encouraged in the New Testament for group worship.[3] Vigorous congregational singing has potent physiological, mental, and spiritual effects. When vigorous congregational singing continues for some time, it encourages a feeling of unity among the singers. Vigorous congregational singing is our fullest expression of corporate worship.

The fact that select choirs or instrumental music are not encouraged in the New Testament doesn't necessarily mean they shouldn't be used in worship services, but does suggest that they should not be seen as preferable to congregational singing.

When we sing vigorously, we breathe deeper and we exercise our chest, back, and abdominal muscles. This floods our cells with extra oxygen, making us feel alert, strong, and energetic. It also releases naturally occurring substances in our brains that relax us, decrease sensitivity to pain, give us a feeling of well-being, encourage

---

[2] One of the most memorable evenings of my life was spent in a hymn-sing led by a man who knew how to lead singing (Charles L. Brooks, an editor of the hymnal I use) and a pianist who knew how to accompany hymn-singing (his daughter). The leader took us through dozens of songs, helping us learn how to sing, how to understand the songs, how to enjoy them. As he moved us from anthems of praise to quiet songs of contrition and surrender and back again, as he gauged and controlled our enthusiasm, we coalesced. I began with a migraine headache. I ended feeling wonderful. This was my introduction, 15 years ago, to the glory of hymns and the physiological effects they can have.

[3] The heavenly choirs of the redeemed seem to include everyone, so they are less choir than congregation. The instruments they play seem to be for accompaniment.

a feeling of compassion for others, and lower our inhibitions slightly (making it easier for us to respond to the work of the Holy Spirit on our hearts).

Meanwhile, the lyrics of songs build our faith, urge us to witness, and help us praise God.

In most worship services there is very little truly corporate worship, with the entire congregation worshiping out loud at the same time.

Too often what is called worship is essentially a spectator sport. We listen to a scripture reading, a prayer, a call for the offering, perhaps a children's story, "special music," a sermon, a benediction.

We can do this without being involved, with our mind focused on other things. When the congregation sings, however, it can sing together.

Most hymns should be sung vigorously, faster and with a stronger emphasis on the beat than is generally done. However, once the congregation is warmed up, the blood flowing, there are slower songs that can have a potent spiritual effect. When hymns are sung more slowly, there is time for people to sing harmony.

Singing a cappella is especially conducive to singing harmony, and when we sing harmony, we have to sing together. (Singing in harmony depends on having a bit of training, but it doesn't require that one sing the notes in the hymnal. There are other good harmonies to be sounded out. The harmonies used in the shape note tradition of *The Sacred Harp* seem discordant to many ears, but they soon come to sound beautiful, and they have spiritual power. I'd love to see congregations taught to sing a cappella from *The Sacred Harp*.)

Vigorous singing, however, does not necessarily mean spiritual singing. Sometimes it is simply vigorous, with no sense of the Spirit, and in that case it's primarily good exercise.

Some of the most spiritual singing I've experienced has been among people gathered for the Lord's Supper, their hearts prepared, spontaneously singing such slow songs as "Just as I Am," "I Surrender All," and "Amazing Grace."

5. Tepid congregational singing is false worship, a mockery of worship. It says, in effect, "God hasn't done much for me and doesn't really deserve my worship."

Tepidness in singing often reflects spiritual lukewarmness, though not necessarily.

Whether lukewarm or simply quiet, the physiological, psychological, and spiritual benefits of wholehearted congregational singing simply aren't experienced by those who don't join in. This means they receive less personal benefit from the worship service. It also means they have less to offer to others and to God.

Those who don't sing vigorously with heart and voice miss out on much of the feeling of unity available to those who sing together.

There are some, it is true, who are so tone-deaf or otherwise impaired that they disrupt the service if they sing. This is a disability, and people with disabilities need special care and extra support and understanding. It is sometimes possible to find some other way to include them in the worship experience.[4]

It is up to the leaders of the worship service to encourage vigorous congregational singing. This can be done by explaining how singing affects people. It can also be encouraged by having talented song leaders. Leading songs effectively in worship requires not only some musical training and enthusiasm, but spiritual maturity and an ability to sense the congregation's spiritual and emotional needs and choose music and make comments that fill them.

I have often heard organists kill congregational unity by playing hymns too slow or even too fast. This decreases unity by frustrating

---

[4] I've mentioned that while for quite a few years I couldn't bring myself to sing praise songs, I enjoyed accompanying them on the guitar. Music therapists working in nursing homes have found that people who can't carry a tune can often carry a rhythm with a tambourine or rhythm sticks, and so be included. Perhaps the tone deaf could provide a steady monotone drone or hum, rather like the drone of a bagpipe or dulcimer (this suggestion is partially tongue in cheek). On the other hand, I've often been dismayed when a congregation begins clapping along with a song—not because the clapping is inappropriate, but because they generally clap out of time. (Actually, people who listen to a lot of popular music often have a better sense of rhythm than many churchgoers. Fortunately, people can learn to clap in time.)

the singers. When organists fail to keep regular time, extending notes longer than the music on the page shows, they can also throw off the congregation.

(True, there are some songs for which congregations are accustomed to extending certain notes, and in this case *not* extending them can cause confusion. However, singing songs slowly and extending notes works best with a cappella singing.)

Some organists like to include "reharmonizations" when they play hymns. This is often very impressive, and it can lead the congregation to greater enthusiasm, but if the reharmonization is too discordant or loses track of the melody, the audience can be confused.

If the organist plays too quietly, people sing less vigorously, and this is not desirable. However, if the organist plays too loudly, it can be difficult to hear one's own voice, and this too is a problem.

Christianity Today columnist Andy Crouch makes some interesting comments on musical volume in his article "Amplified Versions" (April 22, 2002, p. 86), though he is dealing with a serious problem with what I call "rock 'n' roll church," rather than with overly loud organs. He writes, "At its best, amplified music is to sound what a cathedral is to stone; an expression of the timeless longing to build something greater than ourselves, pointing to Someone greater still.

"But I am troubled by many amplified worship services. Next time you're in one of these settings, watch and listen to the congregation. Get ready for the sound of silence. If the sheer volume of amplified worship is like a sonic cathedral, it can also trump the most forbidding medieval liturgy in its capacity to stun churchgoers into a passive stupor. . . . In the face of amplified worship, most congregations don't do much more than clap, close their eyes, and sway a little. . . . When you can't hear yourself singing, why even try?"

I don't have enough experience with this kind of church service to judge whether the problem is as common as he claims. I suspect many worship leaders would think he is exaggerating. However, I think he is right to the extent that whether the high decibels come from an organ or a band, if they discourage unified participation, limiting participants to those with microphones and instruments and talent, they both squelch true worship and set up what Crouch calls "a new priesthood . . . the amplified people [who] do for us what we cannot do for ourselves: make music, offer prayers, approach the unapproachable." True worship should come from brothers and sisters coming together in unity (Ps. 133:1).

Tepid singing is not only a problem with hymns. I attend a church that has about 200 teenagers in the pews. We often sing praise songs in church, and we do it because that's supposed to be what the teenagers like. Yet often the teenagers sing them with no more enthusiasm than the older people exhibit (not much). This makes me wonder why we bother.

The interesting thing is that I've also heard the same group of teenagers sing the same songs in the same room when there are few adults around. Then they sing with enthusiasm and with pleasure, and with about four times the volume. I'm not sure why this is—it seems almost as if they're trying to punish the adults for making them come to church.

What I do know is that teenagers who want livelier worship services should take the first step by singing as if they were alive, whatever the song may be.

6. Vigorous congregational singing is always appropriate during the worship service, and many musical styles are acceptable for such worship, so long as those present are not offended. Music that offends some in the congregation is not acceptable, because it destroys the unity of the body of Christ.

When young people complain about singing "the old hymns," it is usually, I think, because they associate them with the dismal, joyless singing they are used to hearing in church, singing they rightly recognize as a sort of blasphemy.

Thus the pressure for new music in the worship service is primarily the fault of those who didn't sing the old hymns with fervor. The good news is that it's not too late to teach tepid singers to sing vigorously, and it's not too late to show young people that hymns, properly sung, are wonderfully fulfilling and too great to be neglected.

Should there be a place in the worship service for music written by people who are still alive? Yes, there should. We should keep in mind, however, that singing contemporary Christian music in worship is not a guarantee of great singing and spiritual unity.

Those who sing hymns tepidly are quite capable of doing the same with contemporary songs. I have often seen praise songs slaughtered by pianists or organists who despise the songs and seem to mangle the tempo or the beat deliberately.

The primary determinant of the appropriateness of music for worship (apart from the lyrics) should be whether or not the audience is offended. This calls for compromise—not a compromise of principles, but a willingness to put the needs of others before our own needs.

I do *not* mean by this only that older people need to loosen up and let young people do what they want. I also mean that younger people need to learn to appreciate what their elders enjoy.

Young people need to be willing to learn to love the old songs if they expect the older people to learn to like the newer songs. This surrender of self for the good of others is at the heart of the Christian ideal.

If a congregation can achieve unity and praise God with their hearts while a Christian rock band accompanies the singing, then God accepts that worship with joy, I think.[5] If a congregation is simply entertained by the band, however, and doesn't achieve unity or sense a connection with God, then something is wrong, and the worship team needs to reconsider its approach.

If some in the congregation can't bear the music, then the music is destroying the unity of the body of Christ.

The same warnings go for singing praise songs during the wor-

---

[5] Some tell me this is impossible—God cannot accept Christian rock music as a part of worship. If this is true, let them prove it by the Bible.

ship service. They also apply to singing traditional hymns. Where offense is given, there is a need for either change or education.

Some have applied to music Paul's teaching in Romans 14 regarding our duty to give up permissible food if we risk offending "the weaker brother." Who, though, is the weaker brother? Should we refrain from using, say, a bass guitar in worship music because it would offend a family of ultraconservatives who have been church members for 50 years, on the basis that they are weaker brothers with tender consciences?

It seems to me that for Paul, weaker brothers are those who are new in the faith and do not yet understand the freedom that is theirs in Christ Jesus. The old ultraconservatives, unable to compromise their tastes and habits, even if it means winning one more for the kingdom of God, are more like the Pharisees Jesus so frequently condemns.

I prefer to apply to these people the words of Jesus in Matthew 23:15: "Woe to you, scribes and Pharisees, hypocrites! For you cross sea and land to make a single convert, and you make the new convert twice as much a child of hell as yourselves" (NRSV). Those who have been in the church for years should be strong, not weak. They need to be willing to sacrifice self to serve others.

The congregation should sing what doesn't offend most members, but some members may need to be taught that compromising one's tastes is not the same as compromising one's principles.

Also, some people may base their lives on principles that are not in fact biblical, but are drawn from other sources. This sometimes leads to a cultlike mentality and an unbiblical emphasis on character perfection as the means of salvation, rather than on growth in holiness as part of one's personal *evidence* of a continuing walk with God.

Perhaps we need a sort of worship rating system. Then people offended by a certain kind of music could avoid services in which it is found.

7. Some Christian songs are appropriate for outside the worship service, yet not for congregational singing. Songs for congregational singing should praise God in some way or

teach and admonish the congregation. They should have lyrics that are fitting for many people to sing at once, rather than focusing on individual experience. Their tunes should also be melodic, as this makes them easier to sing and remember.

A large percentage of CCM has lyrics more suitable for personal than corporate singing. Many musicians write about their search for God, their struggle to maintain their relationship with God, their doubts and fears, their attempts (often failed) to do what Jesus would do. Sometimes they write about relationships with other people, loneliness, longing, love of nature, work, marriage, or parenting, with little if any explicit Christian content.

These are legitimate topics that deserve exploration by Christians. The lyricists are often dealing with problems faced by many in their audience. We gain strength when we hear others sing about our problems, even if we aren't always presented with the gospel as an answer to the problems.

However, these songs simply don't work very well in corporate worship. The expected pronoun for corporate worship is "we." When "I" occurs too often, it can come to sound self-centered rather than God-centered or body of Christ-centered.[6]

(I don't agree with those who say we shouldn't sing praise songs because the word "I" occurs too often, though we might do well to consider the focus of songs as we choose what to sing.)

For corporate worship we do better to sing songs expressing corporate praise, corporate supplication, corporate needs, corporate faith, and corporate hope, whatever the music that accompanies the lyrics.

Praise songs often have simple melodies, but they are singable melodies. Most popular hymns have singable melodies.[7]

---

[6] This is part of why I don't like to sing that favorite hymn "In the Garden." It's too personal (and, of course, sappy). Even a song like "How Great Thou Art," though not sappy, might be better with less of "I" and "my" and more of "we" and "our."

[7] The hymnbook I use is full of very singable hymns, though some of the songs are trite (and some of the modern hymns included are only marginally spiritual). However, I have heard some truly uninspired melodies in churches in England and in Lutheran and Catholic services (though some are excellent). Boring melodies don't encourage vigorous singing.

One problem I've noticed with transferring rock-type or folk-type CCM to the worship setting is that the melody is sometimes minimal, hovering around one note and seldom going more than a step above or below it. For example, the Jars of Clay song "Flood," though it has a powerful message, works well as a song played and sung by a band, and was a big hit, has a melody with about four notes, and much of the chorus uses only two notes. I've heard groups of people try to sing this, but it simply doesn't work. In the head the song is fine, but there's no melody worth whistling aloud, and it's difficult for a congregation to sing a song that alternates between two notes and doesn't regularly reach a melodic resolution.

What sounds good in a band with one singer sounds like a monotone drone sung by a congregation. When choosing music, we need to consider not only message but melody, whatever the musical style may be.

Conclusion

Musical style is generally a matter of taste, not right or wrong, apart from music that makes us feel angry, frightened, lustful, or some other ungodly feeling, and so should be avoided. However, because above all the church needs to be unified, we need to be ready to compromise our own preferences for the sake of the body of Christ.

We do better to train people than to force them. If a church can't agree on music, it's better to split a church physically into separate congregations than to split it spiritually by imposing the tastes of one faction on another.

Because congregational worship isn't true worship unless the congregation worships as one, and because congregational singing not only helps us achieve that unity but is the primary way the church worships at one time, we need to devote more time to learning how to sing together, and we need to devote more time to singing together.

We need to surrender ourselves to the good of the whole body and sing with our hearts. I believe this is the worship God desires, rather than a worship that is decorous and reverent, but dead.

Chapter 5

What About *The Christian &
Rock Music?* A Review

So the builders built the temple of the Lord.
And the priests stood arrayed in their vestments,
with musical instruments and trumpets,
and the Levites, the sons of Asaph, *with cymbals,*
praising the Lord and *blessing him,*
according to the directions of King David of Israel;
they *sang hymns,* giving thanks to the Lord,
"For his goodness and his glory are forever upon all Israel."
And *all the people sounded trumpets*
and shouted with a great shout,
praising the Lord for the erection of the house of the Lord.
Some of the levitical priests and heads of ancestral houses,
old men who had seen the former house,
came to the building of this one with outcries and loud weeping,
while *many came with trumpets and a joyful noise,*
so that the people could not hear the trumpets
because of the weeping of the people.
For *the multitude sounded the trumpets loudly,*
so that the sound was heard far away;
and when the enemies of the tribe of Judah and Benjamin heard it,
they came to find out what the sound of the trumpets meant.
They learned that those who had returned from exile
were building the temple for the Lord God of Israel.
—1 Esdras 5:58-67, NRSV (cf. Ezra 3:10-13)

Books by Christians opposed to rock music
have been coming out for 40 years. I remember when the Beatles
first visited America. I knew their names and faces from articles in

Life magazine, even though, with no access to a radio, I did not hear their music until several years later.

Before I heard their music, I heard that I shouldn't listen to it because my heart would synchronize with the beat. This synchronization would make my heart beat faster than normal. As I look back on this argument, I know there's a certain truth to it. But now I have the sense to ask, "Why is that a problem?" My heart speeds up when I sit up in the morning or walk up the stairs. My heart is designed to do that. It's normal.

In the 1970s and 1980s there was a flood of books revealing the real or imagined problems of rock music. These were sometimes true, but often sensationalistic, exaggerated, and even built on half-truths.

There was a serious tendency to quote and understand literalistically what was said ironically by musicians. Supermarket tabloids were cited as reliable sources. False claims were passed from book to book. People with no scientific training were cited as "research scientists" on the cutting edge because they'd made some daring claim supposedly based on research.

Because there was virtually no Christian rock in those days, few of the books mentioned it. In the nineties Christian rock began to draw criticism from these authors as well.

Because the Christian musicians, though fallible like the rest of us, pretty much kept their noses clean, those opposing them used guilt by association as their primary weapon. The Christian musicians might not be satanic or promiscuous or drug users, but because some secular musicians were, the Christians too were tarred and branded.

Big Sales and Big Influence

In 2000 Samuele Bacchiocchi self-published *The Christian & Rock Music*.[1] The sales and profits have been surprisingly good for a self-published book. The book includes seven chapters by

---

[1] Samuele Bacchiocchi, ed., *The Christian & Rock Music: A Study on Biblical Principles of Music* (Berrien Springs, Mich: Biblical Perspectives, 2000).

Bacchiocchi, two by Calvin M. Johansson, and one each by Brian Neumann, Eurydice V. Osterman, Günter Preuss, Tore Sognefest, and Wolfgang H. M. Stefani.[2] In this chapter I will examine Bacchiocchi's claims. In the next chapter I will look at the claims of some of the others.

Bacchiocchi has published some outstanding work on the New Testament and church history that I cite and praise in my Bible classes. I wish I could praise this book, but I can't. It has all the problems found in the anti-rock tirades of the seventies and eighties mentioned above (not surprising, as it mines them for information).

If the book had drawn no attention, I would not comment on it, because I don't like to say negative things about a book, especially a friend's book. However, it has had so much influence that young people, parents, and church leaders frequently ask me what I think of it. I believe its influence is damaging relationships by leading to tensions between the young and their elders.

In this chapter I will review *The Christian & Rock Music* by presenting a series of quotations from the book—more or less in the order they are found there—and commenting on them. My comments will suggest what I consider to be a more appropriate way of dealing with the issue.

I hope these comments will lead to healing, to learning to tolerate the praising of God in ways we ourselves don't enjoy, to worship renewal and personal renewal, and to better relationships between parents and children, closer walks with God, and more effective evangelistic witness.

Keavin Hayden includes an excellent chapter on music in his book *Lifestyles of the Remnant* (Hagerstown, Md.: Review and Herald Pub. Assn., 2001). It deserves to be quoted at length here, as his valuable insights differ from my own. "How do we determine

---

[2] Bacchiocchi has been a professor of religion at Andrews University. Johansson teaches music at Evangel University, and Osterman teaches music at Oakwood College. Stefani and Preuss (whose first name is misspelled Güenter in the book) have both written dissertations on church music. Sognefest and Neumann have both been musicians in rock bands.

what is appropriate music for Christians to listen to? Actually, the heart of this question identifies the real core of the answer. *In general, we don't determine which music is appropriate or not appropriate for others.* God has set it up through the liberty of individual conscience that ultimately all must decide for themselves what is the right music for them. That's because different music affects different minds in different ways. Music that leads you to think godly thoughts may prompt devilish ones in me. If I judge you according to my experience, then am I not playing the role of God in your life?

"It is a serious issue, because like most other lifestyle standards it falls into the arena of religious liberty. Before God, each individual has certain 'unalienable rights,' one of which is to worship God according to the dictates of his or her own conscience, not according to the conscience of someone else. And since music is a form of worship, my right to listen to whatever I desire is guaranteed me not only by my nation's government, but by the government of heaven as well.

"Numerous musical gurus will disagree with me. They see it as dangerous to advocate religious liberty in the area of music. To their way of thinking, the suggestion that people should determine for themselves what is good or bad music borders on infidelity. They are more comfortable if they can publicly dictate to our people their understanding of what is safe to listen to and what is not. But I'm telling you, this is nothing short of spiritual dictatorship! . . . No doubt such misguided zeal . . . will actually increase division among church members" (pp. 77, 78).

The genesis of *The Christian & Rock Music* illustrates the thinking behind the book. It began when Bacchiocchi visited Australia in October of 1999. He had been invited to attend a church camp meeting and speak in the Connections tent (age 30 and up) for a week. The night before he was to speak, however, a Christian band played a concert in that tent. As he describes it: "For the first one hour, from 7:30 to 8:30 p.m., they played and sung jazzy, night club type of music, with various percussion instruments. The men of singing group on the platform were jumping up and down as if it were a nightclub performance. In all my travels across the USA I have never witness such a heavy beat, night club type of music, even in the so-called 'celebration churches.'"[3]

He was so offended that he refused to speak in that venue if such music was played. The next day the music planned was canceled, so he spoke, but after that he was replaced and given another venue at a different time. He began speaking against this music, and the response was so positive that he decided he should write a book about how Christians should respond to the use of this music for supposedly sacred purposes.

Bacchiocchi maintains an extensive e-mail list-serve of people interested in his work, as well as a Web site (www.biblicalperspectives.com). When my name was added to the list-serve there were, as I recall, some 6,000 people on his list, and there are now more than 20,000. Bacchiocchi sends e-mails telling where he's been speaking and will be speaking, giving his take on current affairs in society and the church, sharing early drafts of his latest work, and offering special discounts on his books.

Because I receive these e-mails, I heard about the Australia experience a few days after it happened, and I was among those who received and read the chapters of *The Christian & Rock Music* as they were written. In the e-mail quoted above, Bacchiocchi solicited our comments: should he or should he not write about music in the church.

I sent him an e-mail (Nov. 4, 1999) pleading with him to drop the project. I told him I didn't think he had enough firsthand experience with rock music, didn't know enough about it, to write such a book. I told him he seemed to be using the same questionable arguments used for many years.

He responded by e-mail that he was reading many books on the

---

[3] From *Endtime Issues* 29 (Oct. 17, 1999), available at www.biblicalperspectives.com/endtimeissues/eti_29.html. Other issues of the newsletter dealing with music or printing early drafts of chapters found in the book are numbers 30 and 33-41. These are all available on the Web site. As Bacchiocchi's e-mail newsletters are unedited, there are a number of writing errors. These should not be held against him.

topic. What's more, professional musicians would be writing some of the chapters. Having read the published book and having found what I expected, its popularity leads me to respond.[4]

Quotes and Comments

Before commenting on a series of quotations from *The Christian & Rock Music,* I'd like to mention several points on which I think Bacchiocchi and I would agree.

It is true that some rock stars live lives of sin and excess, though not all do. It is true that the lyrics of many rock songs extol the pleasures of various sinful acts (this is also true of country-western songs, show tunes, and even the ballads of centuries past).[5] Even those lyrics that don't celebrate sin may be problematic, because they focus the mind on secular things, such as romance, instead of on God and our search for Him and walk with Him.[6]

Maintaining a walk with God over a lifetime is so difficult that we should consider leaving behind anything that threatens it. In this light, "neutral" lyrics, like "harmless" television and reading and sports, may actually threaten our relationship with God by stealing from us the time we need to keep it fresh.

I want to make it clear that while I will argue in this chapter and the next that most styles of music can be used with lyrics that praise God, and by so doing lead people to God and keep them with God,

---

[4] I sent Dr. Bacchiocchi a copy of an earlier version of this review before it was published. He refused to read it (e-mail to the author, August 28, 2002).

[5] Consider, for example, the many old English or Scottish ballads with gentle tunes but lyrics dealing with adultery, violence, or magic. Even when the lyrics show the negative effects of these things—and they often do, providing a positive moral dimension—they still keep the mind on worldly things rather than on spiritual things.

[6] Note the qualification "may be." It's true that the dichotomy between sacred and secular is in a sense false, as every aspect of our lives should be permeated with God's presence. The fourth commandment tells us to labor six days a week, but we are not told to exclude God from those days. We can be with God in the midst of romance, as we mow the lawn, or as we earn our livings. Certainly these are all topics Christian musicians could sing about. However, if our goal is to avoid sin by clinging to God, then we should recognize that some subjects don't help us do that. They may not be sinful, yet they may not be especially helpful when we are tempted.

I think Christians would do well to turn away from any music with secular lyrics, or at least limit themselves to small doses of secular lyrics that are not problematic for Christians.[7]

Bacchiocchi writes, "Listeners to religious rock will never be humbled by the majesty of God, nor will they be convicted of God's moral claims upon their lives" (p. 30). This is a rather bold claim.

The fact is, I know many who listen to religious rock who have been "humbled by the majesty of God" and admit his "moral claims upon their lives." They sit in my classes. They sat in Bacchiocchi's classes, too, though I'm not sure he realized it.

It's a brave thing to make such a claim. It's the equivalent of stating ex cathedra that "listeners to religious rock" will not be saved. I'm not sure humans have that power before God.

What should we do with a statement like this? "The Sabbath teaches us to respect the distinction between the *sacred* and the *secular,* not only in time, but also in such areas as church music and worship. To use secular music for the church service on the Sabbath is to treat the Sabbath as a secular day and the church as a secular place" (p. 36).

The distinction between the sacred and the secular is much stressed in Bacchiocchi's book, but the Bible says, "The earth is the Lord's, and the fullness thereof" (Ps. 24:1; 1 Cor. 10:28). That makes it harder to separate the sacred from the secular, because the sacred reaches out to the secular and permeates it. Does the opposite hold true as well? Do we despoil the sacred by singing sacred songs on secular days? *"This* is the day the Lord has made" (Ps. 118:24, NIV).

I'm not arguing that we should sing secular songs on the Sabbath, but wondering if there are "secular" days of the week, or even if Christians should be singing secular songs on any day. Besides, the only people I know who approve of secular songs on the Sabbath are those who, like Calvin Johansson, think "serious music" without

---

[7] For example, my grandmother used to love to watch *The Lawrence Welk Show* on Saturday nights. This is an exceptionally clean-cut show, of course, and none of the songs have lyrics that might make a grandmother blush. On the other hand, could that time have been better spent reading the Bible or some devotional book?

words is appropriate for worship simply because it's "great," even if it is written by those who deny God or live lives of sin.

I don't know of anyone who likes Christian rock who thinks we should sing the Rolling Stones' song "Dancin' With Mr. D" as the opening hymn. To insinuate that those who like CCM might do that is like an attempt to win an argument using false statistics.

A number of times in *The Christian & Rock Music* Bacchiocchi makes inferences based on misreadings of biblical texts. He writes, for example: "Twice in Daniel 3 there is a long list of the different musical instruments used to produce 'every kind of music' (Dan. 3:7, 10). . . . Could it be that, as in ancient Babylon, Satan is using today 'every kind of music' to lead the world into the endtime false worship of the 'beast and its image' (Rev. 14:9)? Could it be that a Satanic stroke of genius will write Gospel songs that will have the marking of every taste of music: folk music, jazz, rock, disco, country-western, rap, calypso? Could it be that many Christians will come to love this kind of Gospel songs because they sound very much like the music of Babylon?" (p. 37). This implies that one of the reasons the three Hebrew worthies did not bow to the image in the plain of Dura was that "every kind of music" was playing.

Nothing in Daniel 3 leads us to think the musical instruments were the problem, or even the way they were played. The problem was in bowing in worship to an image of anything or anyone. There is no evidence that Satan was using these instruments because they tend to lead people into false worship in and of themselves.

By definition, "gospel songs" are meant to lead people to Christ, not to Satan. To suggest a relationship between pagan worship and gospel songs is an example of the rhetorical fallacy of non sequitur. Rhetorical fallacies often convince people to accept ideas, whether true or false, but they convince through false argument, not through clearly presenting the evidence. (I do not suggest that any of the authors in this book have deliberately tried to deceive their readers. Rather, I think they failed to think through the logical implications of some of their assertions. Most rhetorical fallacies are used accidentally.)

As I will show later on, there are some substantial contradictions in the book. At some points plainsong (without harmony or rhythm) is praised, while at other points rock music is blasted for not maintaining a balance between melody, harmony, rhythm, and tone or for not being sufficiently "serious" or difficult. Bacchiocchi writes, for example: "The solemn, awe-inspiring music of the early church [such as Gregorian chant (p. 50)] was driven by a lofty view of God. Its avoidance of the secular associations that musical instruments might bring is particularly relevant to the current debate over the use of music and instruments associated with the rock scene" (p. 51).

Is he saying here that we shouldn't use musical instruments in worship because they have "secular associations"? No, he is saying we shouldn't use instruments "associated with the rock scene." But what instruments used in churches are not also used in rock music? The piano and organ are staple instruments in rock music! He admiringly quotes Lois Ibsen Al Faruqi, who writes, of early Christian and Islamic music, "Performance practice, relying on the human voice, has avoided the secular associations which instruments might bring, as well as the chordal harmonies which could be suggestive of emotional or dramatic effects. Even the use of the human voice or voices . . . has avoided the sensual and imitative in order to enhance the spiritual effect on the listener" (p. 51).

Are we then to oppose harmony in the church, or the use of chords? Plainsong was and still is highly conducive to trance states, even though beat-free and drawing words from the Psalms. Also, as with today's charismatic worshipers, the sense of God moving in the person was very important among the monastics.

We see here the rhetorical fallacy of "special pleading." Instruments used to play the music Bacchiocchi dislikes are not acceptable because they are "associated with the rock scene," but the same instruments are acceptable if they play music he likes. If he were to argue that no instruments should be used at all, he would at least be consistent.

Of course, given that Bacchiocchi is best known for his excellent book *From Sabbath to Sunday,* showing the influence of the early

Roman church on the change in the day of worship, it's interesting that he would recommend to us the example of Catholic monks.

It is said that the proof of the pudding is in the tasting. Similarly, Jesus said, "By their fruits ye shall know them" (Matt. 7:20, KJV). Bacchiocchi, it seems, prefers another cliché: The apple never falls far from the tree. He writes, "If the church uses a rock type of music, which is associated with sex, drugs, satanism, violence, and the rejection of the Christian faith, it obviously is not able to challenge the youth to live up to the moral claims of the Gospel" (p. 97).

He assumes that if secular rock has these associations, Christian rock must as well. This is a bit like saying that because some cultures combined worship and prayer with prostitution, we should not worship and pray to God.

The fact is, Christian rock music has proved over and over that it is "able to challenge the youth to live up to the moral claims of the Gospel." In fact, the type of CCM I least enjoy, Christian rap, proves to be the most hard-hitting in its challenge—much harder than most preachers I've heard.[8]

Guilt by association is a long-used tool for controlling people and stifling what may be a harmless style. I remember being told in academy, as a teenager, that Christians shouldn't wear blue jeans because that's what rock musicians and drug users wore.[9] Similar arguments are still being used. Bacchiocchi writes: "Can rock music, which in the sixties rejected Christianity, glorified sexual perversion, and promoted drugs which claimed the lives of some of its heroes, be legitimately transformed into a fitting medium to worship God and proclaim the Gospel's message? In answering this question, it is important to remember that *the medium affects the message*. If the medium is associated with the rejection of Christianity, sexual per-

---

[8] For example, the group from Philadelphia called the Cross Movement.

[9] I responded by dyeing my blue jeans black. That was acceptable (except to my mother, who objected to everything else in the washing machine turning black). I was amused to find, when I attended my thirtieth class reunion a few months ago, that today the teachers and the principal wear blue jeans to work if they want. Good for them!

version, and drugs, it cannot be legitimately used to communicate the moral claims of the Gospel" (p. 84).

The medium of television, the medium of books, and the medium of magazines are all associated with "the rejection of Christianity, sexual perversion, and drugs," yet Christians use them all to spread the gospel, consecrating them to the work of Christ.

A number of previous musical styles—some now considered "serious music"—were to some extent associated with sex and drug use or considered risqué or dangerous. Recall, for example, some of the romantic composers of the nineteenth century,[10] or the opera, or the waltz. Haydn's tune used for the German national anthem,[11] "Deutschland über alles"—made notorious during the Nazi period—is now the tune of a favorite hymn, "Glorious Things of Thee Are Spoken."

If we must believe that secular connotations negate the spiritual force of sacred music, we would do well not to forget the first (and last) two lines of the second verse of this anthem: "Deutsche Frauen, deutsche Treue, / Deutscher Wein und deutscher Sang."[12]

What makes a book worth citing? Is it scholarly accuracy, or first-hand authority, or is it salacious rumor-mongering? Bacchiocchi writes: "In his book *Dancing With Demons*, Jeff Godwin gives startling evidence on a number of popular rock musicians who have studied the ancient beat of satanic worship. These rockers include Brian Jones (Rolling Stones), John Phillips (Mamas and Papas), and Paul McCartney (Beatles). These men have studied with satanic masters in order to learn how to use effectively the hypnotic power of the rock beat in their songs" (p. 89).

One anonymous reviewer at Amazon.com seems right in claim-

---

[10] Among those whose work I've heard played in church, Berlioz is said to have written a symphony while using opium, Schubert was a heavy drinker and had syphilis, Chopin and Liszt are notorious for their sex lives, and Brahms got his start in music playing in bars and brothels.

[11] The words were written in 1841; Haydn wrote the tune in 1797 for an Austrian patriotic song honoring the emperor, "Gott, erhalte Franz, den Kaiser."

[12] "German women, German fidelity, / German wine and German song."

ing that Jeff Godwin is "much given to misinterpretation, misquoting, general cluelessness, and outright lies." His approach is to find satanic conspiracies everywhere in rock music, on the flimsiest of evidence, such as supermarket tabloids.

This is typical of many of the sources quoted in *The Christian & Rock Music*. None of the three men mentioned above were drummers. Jones was known for introducing the marimba, the dulcimer, the recorder, and the harpsichord to rock music. Phillips is best known for "California Dreamin'" and McCartney for "Yesterday." Ancient satanic beats? Hardly.

Bacchiocchi writes, "The defining characteristic of good music is a balance among three basic elements: melody, harmony, and rhythm" (p. 129). Wouldn't this mean that early church music, which didn't use harmony or rhythm, was unbalanced? Does the balance have to be exact? What about an a cappella solo performance of a hymn?

It seems that by Bacchiocchi's definition, such a performance could not possibly be "good music." He adds, "Rock music inverts this order by making rhythm its dominant element, then harmony, and last melody." If they are balanced, though, then they are equal, so there is no order to be inverted.

However, why is it necessarily wrong to have rhythm stronger than harmony or melody at times? Surely there are a great many instances of "great music" in which this is the case.

When people make categorical statements defining "good music," they often open themselves to ridicule. Bacchiocchi is no exception. He writes: "In any good piece of music, the strongest beat in a pattern (measure) is the downbeat (the first beat in the pattern). If a pattern has four beats, the strongest [in "good" music] is the first, and the second strongest beat is the third, . . . Rock music reverses the common order of the beat by placing the emphasis on what is known as the offbeat. In the offbeat, the main emphasis falls on beat four and the secondary beat is on beat two" (p. 131).

It is true that the usual definition of a downbeat is the accentuated first beat in a measure, or the first and third beat of a measure in 4/4, while an upbeat is generally defined as the unaccented second and fourth beats of a measure in 4/4.

However, this is actually arbitrary: the first beat in the measure is stressed because that's the way composers have been taught to do it. Does this mean that melodies always begin with a stressed note? Not at all! (Think of "The Lord in Zion Reigneth," in which "Lord" is the first stressed word.)

How, then, does a composer write out a melody that begins with an unstressed beat? The composer begins with an incomplete measure, so the first stressed beat will fall at the beginning of the first complete measure.

The fact is that this works on paper, but our bodies don't have the sheet music. Our bodies recognize the rhythms inherent in songs, not the artificial system of measures. Most people can't read music, but they sense rhythmic patterns and respond to them.

For most people, the notes before the downbeat are part of the entire rhythm. It is true that rock music often (but certainly not always) accentuates the second and fourth beats of the measures, but to some extent this is because the songs are written out by people who haven't learned the "rules" for how to do it right.

Have you ever listened to your heart with a stethoscope? Which comes first, the stressed beat or the unstressed beat (or can you hear more than that)? A cardiologist might be able to tell you, but for most of us, whether our hearts sound like "lub-DUB-lub-DUB" or "LUB-dub-LUB-dub" is a trick of the ear not trained in the physiological facts. What really matters for most of us is not which beat comes first, but that they continue beating.

To show the weakness of Bacchiocchi's assertion—a favorite of anti-rock crusaders for decades—it suffices to consider the *actual* beat in several of our greatest hymns (I am basing this, remember, on how they are sung, not how they may look on the page). "A Mighty Fortress Is Our God" has this "rock" beat. So does "The Old Rugged Cross" (and it is also "anapestic"—a beat condemned in the next chapter). "O Worship the King," "O Word of God Incarnate," and "O Little Town of Bethlehem," among many others, use this beat.

This is the beat in the march "Stars and Stripes Forever" (though not on the sheet music). This is also the beat found in poetry written in iambics (probably 90 percent of metric verse in English)—one reason it's common in hymn settings.

On the other hand, it might be worth mentioning that bluegrass music is characterized by the beat Bacchiocchi requires for "good music" (though with the guitar chords played on the second and fourth beats). I don't know how he feels about bluegrass, but I'm sure his coauthor Calvin Johansson, whose work is discussed in the next chapter, would not consider bluegrass "serious music," as he calls the music he likes.

It is true that there are certain ways of playing this "reversed" beat Bacchiocchi complains about that can make people want to dance, but that in itself is not sinful.[13]

He continues, "The fundamental problem with rock music is its relentless beat which dominates the music and produces an hypnotic effect." It is true that some rock music has a "relentless beat" that can cause a trancelike state (though not literally "hypnotic").

However, many forms of music have a similar effect, when people concentrate on the music to the extent that they tune out what is happening around them, and almost seem to enter the music or have the music enter them.

For example, in orchestral performances of classical music, it is common to see people in the audience with their eyes closed and their hands surreptitiously conducting the music or keeping the beat.

---

[13] One might say I am quibbling here, that Bacchiocchi is talking about deafeningly loud rock 'n' roll drumming, not about the rhythms found in hymns. This may be the case, but he doesn't say so. Instead he categorically condemns a specific rhythm found not only in songs but in poetry. I assert that the inaccuracy of his language makes my comments appropriate and suggests that he hasn't really thought through the implications of his statements. Neither, unfortunately, have many of his readers, judging from the influence the book is having.

At band concerts one often finds people tapping their feet during marches without realizing it.

The Gregorian chant Bacchiocchi celebrates in his book is deliberately designed to induce a trancelike state in which one feels very close to God, and it certainly succeeds, if one is willing to relax one's analytical faculties and surrender to the music.

Experiencing this trancelike state is not in itself necessarily a bad thing. It's pleasurable, relaxing, and not generally harmful. It becomes dangerous when it leads to violence or other sinful activity, or makes one more likely to accept sinful ideas found in song lyrics. But if the words heard during this trancelike state induced by the "relentless beat" of Christian rock are "Lord, I praise You," where's the problem?

Many of us are so rational that we have a very hard time surrendering to any beat, and for us to "lift up holy hands in prayer" (1 Tim. 2:8, NIV) while singing praise songs is unimaginable. But perhaps that is our loss. Why should we impose our own failures on those able to praise God with greater enthusiasm than we ourselves can muster?

Here is another categorical "good music" statement. "Good music follows exact mathematical rules, which causes the mind to feel comforted, encouraged, and 'safe.' Musicians have found that when they go against these rules, the listener experiences an addictive high" (p. 134). Given that the musical scale we use is based on "exact mathematical rules," "bad" music also follows exact mathematical rules, or we wouldn't recognize it as music.

But does "good music" always make us "feel comforted, encouraged, and 'safe'"? The "Dies Irae" ("Day of Wrath") section of Verdi's Requiem is generally considered "good music," but the music is terrifying—fitting for the topic. Beethoven's fifth symphony is generally considered "good music," but it hardly makes one feel "comforted, encouraged, and 'safe.'"

Even jazz and blues music, which "bend" notes away from the strictly mathematical scale (also a feature of Indian and Chinese classical music), achieve their effect only because there *is* a mathematically described scale against which they can push. Furthermore, if "musicians have found that when they go against these rules, the listener experiences an addictive high," then we would all be addicted to atonal music, which is not the case.

Can people grow so fond of music that their lives seem empty without it? Yes, of course, but this isn't quite "an addictive high," and it happens with all types of music.

Do some types of rock music have physical effects that some listeners crave? Yes, but not all types, and not because the music doesn't follow "mathematical rules."

Do some people gravitate toward music that makes them feel depressed, angry, or frightened? Yes, but this doesn't characterize the majority of rock music.

Here's an interesting question: "Ultimately, the question is: *Should church music stimulate people physically or elevate them spiritually?*" (p. 138). The answer is *both,* because they are related. Physical stimulation in moderation makes people more receptive to spiritual influence, putting them in a good mood, with a smile on their face, ready to learn and to hear God's voice.

Bacchiocchi writes, "As Christians, we need to be aware of the fact that music is perceived through the portion of the brain that receives stimuli for sensations and feelings, *without being first screened by the brain centers involving reason and intelligence*" (p. 139). While there may be some truth to this, it's also true that the reason and intelligence immediately set to work on the stimulus, deciding whether they like the music or not, if it's well performed, if mistakes are being made, if the lyrics are true.

Furthermore, this applies to all music, not merely rock music. Consider, for example, the thundering pipe organ in church. Does that affect us? Can some organ music make us feel hopeless or worried? Yes! The fact that such music is "serious" and of a high quality does not mean it is necessarily conducive to worship.

Here's another categorical assertion: "The Christian commitment to Christ leaves no room for Christian artists to cross over into the secular rock scene" (p. 147). This is a little like saying, "The Christian commitment to Christ leaves no room for Christians to associate with non-Christians in order to share God's love with them."

Are there dangers inherent in trying to be a Christian in the "secular rock scene"? Of course! But there are also dangers in going to a foreign land as a missionary. Furthermore, it is also difficult to be a Christian musician performing in secular symphony orchestras. There are tough decisions to make. But people do it.

For biblical scholars, some of the most worrisome of Bacchiocchi's statements are those deriving principles from the Hebrew Temple services, as they have so little relationship to our worship today, and he frequently misinterprets the passages he cites. He writes: "Those who believe that the Bible gives them the license to play any instrument and music in church, ignore the fact that the music at the Temple was not based on personal taste or cultural preferences. This is indicated by the fact that other instruments like timbrels, flutes, pipes, and dulcimers could not be used in the Temple, because of their association with secular entertainment" (p. 178).

Bacchiocchi is basing this comment on 2 Chron. 29:25, referring to the reconsecration of the Temple under Hezekiah. The verse reads, "He stationed the Levites in the house of the Lord with cymbals, harps, and lyres, according to the commandment of David and of Gad the king's seer and of the prophet Nathan, for the commandment was from the Lord through his prophets" (NRSV).

There are a number of problems with Bacchiocchi's statement. First, there is nothing at all in this text or in any associated text (such as 1 Chron. 25:1, 6) that says other instruments couldn't be used because of "their association with secular entertainment." After all, "cymbals, harps, and lyres" were *also* used for secular entertainment.

Second, the text does not say these were to be the instruments used in the Temple for all time. Third, if we assume this command still stands, we must exclude the piano and organ from the worship service. (Certainly the guitar is more like the harp and lyre of David's day than is the organ, and drum sets have cymbals.)

It would be interesting to know more about music in the Temple services, but our lack of knowledge should not be seen as an invitation to invent what is not provided. Bacchiocchi cites admiringly studies by John W. Kleining and A. Z. Idelsohn that claim that in the Temple services the cymbals and trumpets did not accompany the singers, but were used only to introduce songs and mark ends of lines or stanzas (pp. 206, 207).

He claims that only the lyres and harps were used to accompany the singing, citing 2 Chronicles 5:12, 13 as supporting this (p. 207). However, 2 Chronicles 5:13 tells us explicitly that the trumpeters and singers sang and played qōl-'eḥad, "as one" or "in unison." Then it adds that the singing was done "with trumpets and with cymbals and with the instruments of the song" (my own awkward but exact translation).

Note that the word "with," repeated three times, makes it clear that all these instruments *accompanied* the singing and didn't merely indicate stanza or line breaks.

Bacchiocchi writes, "Some argue that if we are to follow the example of the Temple, we need to eliminate in the church such instruments as the piano and the organ, because they are not string instruments. Such an argument ignores the distinction between a biblical principle and its cultural application. The biblical principle is that instrumental music accompanying the singing should aid the vocal response to God and not drown it. . . . Another point is that instruments like the organ or the piano were unknown in Bible times" (p. 209).

This is again the rhetorical fallacy known as "special pleading." Bacchiocchi makes this plea for acceptance of what he approves of on the basis of the "cultural application" of a "biblical principle."

He ignores the fact that the electric bass, keyboard, and drum kit also didn't exist in Bible times. In fact, the organ in some churches does drown the singing.

Also, if people are singing enthusiastically, the instruments may have to get pretty loud before the voices are drowned out. Again, even electric guitars and drums can be played more quietly than the singing of a congregation.

Consider too the singing of heaven. When the huge army of the redeemed sing, they sound "like the roar of a great multitude in heaven shouting," "like the roar of rushing waters and like peals of thunder" (Rev. 19:1, 6).

If they are playing harps at the same time, the harps may need to be electrified if they are to be heard. Then again, "like peals of thunder" sounds rather like a rock concert! Now there's a "joyful noise" I want to hear, and the sooner the better!

If we are to admit 2 Chronicles 29:25 as relevant, then we must go all the way: we must have 288 musicians who play in groups of 12, with each group playing for two weeks a year (1 Chron. 25:6-31). Also, we must have only men in our choirs, and we must put an end to congregational singing. We must also have people assigned to the "ministry of prophesying, accompanied by harps, lyres and cymbals" (1 Chron. 25:1, NIV; verse 3 defines "prophesying" as "thanking and praising the Lord").[14]

In truth, the instruments used in services at Solomon's Temple are completely irrelevant to the question of what instruments we should play today when praising God. The Temple services were very different from church services today, and the function of the Temple was also far different from the function of today's church.

Consider that the primary purpose of the Temple was not worship, but sacrifice. Consider that worshipers could not enter the Temple. They probably couldn't even enter the courtyard.

---

[14] Seeing "prophesying" as "thanking and praising the Lord" may help us understand Saul's "prophesying" in 1 Sam 10:9-12, predicted by Samuel in verses 5-7: "You will meet a band of prophets coming down from the shrine with harp, tambourine, flute, and lyre playing in front of them; they will be in a prophetic frenzy. Then the spirit of the Lord will possess you, and you will be in a prophetic frenzy along with them and be turned into a different person. Now when these signs meet you, do whatever you see fit to do, for God is with you" (NRSV). If God was truly with Saul as he thanked and praised, then Saul's worship must have been acceptable, even though accompanied by a tambourine. Saul's "frenzy," occurring when "the Spirit of God came upon him in power" (verse 10, NIV), seems disturbingly similar to that found in some Holy Roller Pentecostal services.

The Temple was the way God was able to have His presence among His people. It was not a place of communal worship, in general, but a way of segregating God from His people so He didn't destroy them with His holiness. What was appropriate in the Temple, in the presence of God, may not be what is appropriate in our churches today.

Our churches are more like the synagogues of Jesus' day. Whether or not instruments were played in synagogues is immaterial, because the Bible gives us no command about synagogues. If we must do in our churches what was done in the synagogues, then pastors must stand when they read the Scriptures and sit when they explain it.

When we sing "The Lord Is in His Holy Temple," we speak metaphorically. Our bodies are the temple of God today (1 Cor. 6:19), and the body of believers called the church is the temple of God (2 Cor. 6:16). If God is more fully present in the church building than elsewhere, it is only because there are believers gathered together in His name, so there He is (Matt. 18:20).

This makes it much more difficult to distinguish between sacred and secular, because we may defile the temple of God by defiling ourselves, but even so we still *are* that temple. This means we should always be careful what we do or say or listen to.

Bacchiocchi writes, "No 'Jewish' or 'Christian' music concerts were performed by bands or singing artists at the Temple, synagogue, or Christian churches. Religious music was not an end to itself but as a means to praise God by chanting His Word" (p. 193).

He neglects to mention that there were also no sacred concerts of "serious music," either. To be consistent, if Bacchiocchi is right we should no longer sing hymns whose lyrics are not in the Bible. We should not sing in any case, but chant. We should have no more vocal solos, no more instrumental performances without singing.

He adds, "Pleasure in singing comes not from a rhythmic beat that stimulates people physically, but from the very experience of praising the Lord" (p. 193). Actually, "pleasure in singing" can be had from a wide range of music, while much of what passes for "praising the Lord" is far less than enthusiastic or pleasurable.

If *true* pleasure in singing comes when praising God, does that logically mean that this must not be accompanied with "a rhythmic beat"? Most hymns are best sung with "a rhythmic beat."

Indeed, according to Bacchiocchi's definition of "good music" as "a balance among three basic elements: melody, harmony, and rhythm" (p. 129), singing without "a rhythmic beat" cannot be "good music."

He also claims that David's dancing before the Lord (2 Sam. 6:14) led David into serious error. In the excitement of this dance David seems to have removed his royal robes—probably rather hot and heavy—and danced in "a linen ephod."

Bacchiocchi writes, "Nowhere does the Bible suggest that the ephod could be legitimately worn by someone who was not a priest" (p. 226). This is true. However, there is also nowhere where the Bible says a linen ephod is to be worn only by a priest. (Some people say, "What is not specifically allowed is forbidden. Others say, "What is not specifically forbidden is allowed." I believe Christians should be among the latter group.)

We don't really know much about ephods. In some cases they seem to be something used for telling the future or inquiring of God (Judges 8:27; 17:5; 1 Sam. 23:9; Hosea 3:4). More often they are garments worn by the high priest and containing the stones used for inquiring of God. They are also the simple white garments worn by priests. Were they also worn by others? Is ephod a word for the garment worn under the outer robes? We don't know.

But nothing tells us it was only for priests. Bacchiocchi continues, "By offering sacrifices dressed like a priest, David was assuming a priestly role in addition to his kingly status. Such an action cannot be easily defended biblically." How dancing led to this, I'm not sure.

However, when 2 Samuel 6:17, 18 says that David offered sacrifices before God, that does not mean he himself performed the priestly duties. More likely he offered the sacrifices expected of a king, or had them sacrificed for him.

Bacchiocchi also writes, "But it would appear that during the dance, David may have become so excited that he lost his loin cloth" (p. 227). He bases this on the accusation of David's wife Michal in 2 Samuel 6:20.

Given what we know of mores in ancient Israel, it seems highly unlikely that David danced "before the Lord" without his loincloth, or that "any vulgar fellow" (verses 14, 20, NIV) did so. It seems much more likely that Michal was exaggerating, making what was innocent seem perverse and sinful.

Bacchiocchi does the same throughout *The Christian & Rock Music*. In our eagerness to call sin by its right name, we can sometimes label as sinful what is simply different.

Bacchiocchi devotes about 10 pages of his chapter "Biblical Principles of Music" to the relationship between dancing and music (pp. 218-228), though scholars might see his explication not as exegesis but as wriggling away from texts that weaken his thesis. While this chapter is not about dancing but music, this section of his book deserves comment.

The most important texts he needs to deal with are Psalm 149:3 ("Let them praise his name with dancing, making melody to him with tambourine and lyre" [NRSV]), and Psalm 150:4 ("Praise him with tambourine and dance; praise him with strings and pipe!" [NRSV]).

Both "dancing" and "dance" in these verses are from the same word in Hebrew, *māḥôl*. This and the related word *mᵉḥōlâ* are used in two thirds of the references to dancing in the Old Testament. They are the usual, general words for dancing, and they are not used figuratively, but always literally, though for various types of dances, some of which might be used for praising God and some of which would dishonor God.

(Similarly, we use the general word "dance" for classical ballet, the jitterbug, and break dancing, different though they may be from each other.)

Eager to avoid admitting that we can praise God by dancing, Bacchiocchi suggests (fairly) that the noun *māḥôl* may be derived from the verb *ḥûl,* but then quotes the speculation by the eighteenth century commentator Adam Clarke that *ḥûl* means "to make an opening" (that may be the idea behind *ḥûl,* but it is not the meaning of the word). He also emphasizes the dubious marginal note in some KJV Bibles that the word might refer to a pipe. Thus for Bacchiocchi, dancing has been turned to piping.

However, the more authoritative lexicon by Brown, Driver, and Briggs translates *ḥûl* as "whirl, dance, writhe," including writhing in the pains of childbirth. Only two or three times is the word *ḥûl* translated as dance, but it helps us understand the nature of dance in the Old Testament: it whirled and writhed. It was not necessarily stately or balletic. There is no suggestion in Brown, Driver, and Briggs that *ḥûl* might mean piping.

A favorite technique of Bacchiocchi is to call figurative what he doesn't want to be literal. There is some figurative language in Psalms 149 and 150, but not where the dancing is involved. The most important question for him is whether dancing occurred in Solomon's Temple, but I've shown above that for Christians, the Temple ceremonies have nothing to do with the worship service.

Psalm 149:1 seems to indicate that the setting is "in the assembly of the faithful" (NRSV), but of course the "assembly of the faithful" never entered the Temple, and only those who were sacrificing, it seems, could enter the inner courtyard.

Psalm 150:1 says, "Praise God in his sanctuary," but the parallel line says "Praise him in his mighty firmament!" This may suggest that God's true sanctuary is not on earth but in the heavens. Thus neither psalm says beyond doubt that that it is talking about the worship service in the Temple.

Furthermore, "let them sing for joy on their couches" (Ps. 149:5, NRSV) can't possibly refer to the Temple, and verses 6-9 call on God's warriors to praise God while slaughtering their enemies, which again wasn't supposed to be done in the Temple.

It is true that these psalms don't necessarily refer to sanctuary worship, even though Psalm 150 may be speaking of the sort of worship *the people* did outside the Temple, especially on feast days, even if the priests were more restrained.

However, Bacchiocchi has missed the most important implication of these chapters for his thesis: the irrefutable evidence that the psalmist here urges the people, whoever they may be and wherever they are, to *praise* God *while* singing, dancing, playing stringed instruments, wind instruments, and various loud percussion instruments.

Whatever people may have done during worship services at the Temple, the psalmist tells us that praise and dance and percussion instruments go together. Indeed, the word "praise" is in the imperative verb form—a strong urging or even a command.

Whether or not these instruments were all used by Levites in the formal Temple services is beside the point. These psalms clearly suggest that the whole gamut of instruments in the psalmist's day could be used to praise God.

If we want to talk about "biblical principles," *there* is the biblical principle: any instrument today can be used to praise God—even the needle on the record turntable scratched back and forth by rap DJs.

I'm not eager to see "liturgical dance" in the worship service today, but the Bible explicitly calls on believers to praise God while dancing. Last semester I had a Messianic Jew in my Old Testament Literature class, and it turned out that she is the dance instructor for her synagogue. The religious folk dances that are an important part of worship in the Messianic synagogue are fun for the children and draw many people who would otherwise not at first be interested in the message of Messianic Judaism. I'm not urging that we too dance as part of worship, but neither can I biblically condemn those who do.[15]

---

[15] Hayden writes, "What I am trying to do is caution against a witch hunt mentality that would lead us automatically to condemn anything that may savor of something we ourselves are not familiar or comfortable with. We must get over the superstition that if the music makes the toe tap it has to be of the devil. . . . God is not limited to a certain style of a certain age in the past. New and fresh every morning, He has the ability to adapt Himself to the needs of each and every new generation, thus meeting them where they are. While He uses the spiritual classics of the past, He also employs music contemporary to our age to reach today's young people with the message of His love and saving power" (Hayden, *Lifestyles of the Remnant,* p. 80).

Like Calvin Johansson (in the next chapter), Bacciocchi draws from the idea of the unblemished sacrifice the idea of unblemished music, as if making a mistake in a performance were a sin. He writes, "As He required the burnt offerings to be 'without blemish' (Lev. 1:3), so it is reasonable to assume that He expects us to present Him with the very best musical offering. There is no biblical basis for believing that the loud, noise-making music or questionable lyrics are acceptable to God" (p. 198).

Contemporary Christian music is not, of course, known for "questionable lyrics." No one is proposing that "questionable lyrics" be sung in church. If God "expects us to present Him with the very best musical offering," does that mean He wants us to hire professional musicians to play for Him?

If, in order to present "the very best musical offering," we exclude congregational singing and turn to choirs and professional musicians, then we are counting on others to do for us what, since the cross, we ourselves can do.

We don't need an earthly musical mediator to translate our praises into a style God can appreciate any more than we need an earthly priestly mediator to pray for us.

Similarly, I love to hear my children sing God's praises, no matter how out of key they may be.[16] I think God feels the same, even if the music is loud.

Bacciocchi writes: "The frequent references to praising God among the heathens or Gentiles (2 Sam. 22:50; Rom. 15:9; Ps. 108:3) suggest that singing was seen as an effective way to witness for the Lord to unbelievers. However, there are no indications in the Bible that the Jews or the early Christians borrowed secular tunes and songs to evangelize the Gentiles" (p. 198).

This is the rhetorical fallacy known as the "argument from silence." We know nothing about the tunes or songs used "to evan-

---

[16] Which is not to say that they necessarily sing out of key, given that they have all sung for years in a rigorous classical children's chorus.

gelize the Gentiles." We don't even know if songs were used for evangelism, or only to praise God when *among* Gentiles.

(The music scholar Suzanne Haïk-Vantoura believes the Hebrew Old Testament text contains notation allowing the entire Old Testament to be sung, but few Hebrew scholars agree with her.[17] In any case, if her tunes are correct, Old Testament singing was wildly different indeed from both our hymns and the singing in the synagogue today—beautiful, but rarely in stanzaic format. What is more, we don't know the tempo or rhythm with which they were sung. Haik-Ventura believes the songs would have been sung slowly, but they might just as easily have been sung with a strong rhythm, like Jewish folksinging today. If the scales she posits are correct, we might also argue that in light of sacred song in the Old Testament, we should usually sing in minor keys today. I'd rather not.)

If we should try to do things as they were done in the time of Christ, perhaps we should allow no musical instruments at all in church. Bacchiocchi writes, "Apparently Christians followed the tradition of the synagogue in prohibiting the use of musical instruments in their church services because of their pagan association" (p. 216).

Should we do the same? Do our instruments, such as the piano, have any less pagan association? Anyway, where does the New Testament say instruments weren't used in Christian worship because of their pagan association?

This is simply Bacchiocchi's guess, and again it is an example of the rhetorical fallacy of the argument from silence. Perhaps the average person didn't know how to play a musical instrument!

If we follow the Bible, perhaps we should not only have no musical instruments in the church, but also not allow women to take part in worship music. Bacchiocchi has little biblical footing when he opines, "Why were women excluded from the music ministry of

---

[17] Suzanne Haïk-Vantoura, *The Music of the Bible Revealed: The Deciphering of a Millenary Notation,* trans. Dennis Weber (D. & F. Scott, 1991). There are tapes and CDs available of her transcriptions being performed by professional musicians. The music is beautiful, but certainly can't be sung by an untrained congregation.

the Temple, first, and of the synagogue and early church later. . . .
From a musical perspective, the style of music produced by women
had a rhythmic beat which was better suited for entertainment than
for worship in God's House. . . .

"Women's music was largely based on a rhythmic beat produced
by tapping with the hand the tabret, toph, or timbrel. . . . From a
sociological perspective, women were not used in the ministry of
music of the Temple because of the social stigma attached to their
use of timbrel and the entertainment-oriented music. . . .

"The lesson from Scripture and history is *not* that women should
be excluded from the music service of the church today. Praising the
Lord with music is not a male prerogative, but the privilege of every
child of God. It is unfortunate that the music produced by women
in Bible times was mostly for entertainment and, consequently, not
suitable for divine worship" (pp. 228-231).

The Bible does not tell us women were "excluded from the
music ministry" of the Temple, synagogue, or early church. It simply tells us the singers in the Temple were men.

Nothing in the Bible suggests that women did not sing in the
synagogue or early church (which is not the same as proving they
did, of course). Nothing in the Bible tells us women were excluded
from singing because their music "had a rhythmic beat which was
better suited for entertainment than for worship in God's House."
This is mere eisegesis, forcing one's own prejudices onto the text.

In 1 Samuel 18:6 women sing "joyful songs" (NIV) while praising David and Saul, but to call this "entertainment-oriented music"
is misleading. The "lesson from Scripture and history" Bacchiocchi
draws is a non sequitur. Nowhere are we told in Scripture that
women were excluded because they played rhythm instruments. We
simply find no women performing in the Temple.

If there is a lesson we should draw from the Temple in considering our actions today—and I don't think there is, given that
the Temple was not a church as we use the word—then that lesson, logically, is exactly the one Bacchiocchi disavows: we should

have no music by women in the church. If they didn't do it then, we shouldn't do it now.

Essentially, Bacchiocchi's argument is as follows: (1) women didn't sing in the Temple back then; (2) their not singing then is significant for us today; (3) so women *should* sing today, but without singing "women's music." This is not a logical syllogism.

As for women as entertainers, we might consider three great hymns by women: the song of Moses and Miriam (Ex. 15:1-21); the song of Deborah (Judges 5); and the song of Mary[18] (Luke 1:46-55).

The reversed narrative order in Exodus 15 is quite common in Hebrew, but it can mislead English speakers. Following the story of the destruction of the Egyptians in Exodus 14, chapter 15 devotes 18 verses to the song sung by "Moses and the Israelites." Where did that song come from? This is the question readers might ask. We find out in verses 19-21. "Miriam the prophetess," beating a tambourine, and followed by "all the women," also beating tambourines and dancing, sang this great hymn, forebear of the Song of Moses and the Lamb sung in Revelation 15. Miriam sings the song alone, with accompaniment.

Note that in verse 1 "Moses and the Israelites" sing it. Where did they learn it? Surely they didn't all sing it together without ever learning it! The answer is that they learned it from the one who sang alone, from Miriam, its probable author. We see thus that rhythm instruments can be fitting accompaniment to praise given to God.

In the next chapter we will look at some problems with the claims of other authors of *The Christian & Rock Music*.

Meanwhile, what we have studied so far reminds me of a few lines from Shakespeare's great play about justice and mercy, *The Merchant of Venice*:

---

[18] Miriam and Deborah are called prophetesses in the Bible. Mary is not, yet she too speaks prophetically in her song.

"In religion
What damned error, but some sober brow
Will bless it, and approve it with a text,
Hiding the grossness with fair ornament?"

Chapter 6

More About
The Christian & Rock Music

O *clap your hands, all ye people;*
shout unto God with the voice of triumph.
For the Lord most high is terrible;
he is a great King over all the earth.
He shall subdue the people under us,
and the nations under our feet.
He shall choose our inheritance for us,
the excellency of Jacob whom he loved. Selah.
God is gone up *with a shout,*
the Lord *with the sound of a trumpet.*
Sing praises to God, *sing praises:*
sing praises unto our King, *sing praises.*
For God is the King of all the earth:
sing ye praises with understanding.
God reigneth over the heathen:
God sitteth upon the throne of his holiness.
The princes of the people are gathered together,
even the people of the God of Abraham:
for the shields of the earth belong unto God:
he is greatly exalted.
—Psalm 47

Having considered seven chapters by
Samuele Bacchiocchi, we now turn to Tore Sognefest's essay "The
Effects of Rock Music" in *The Christian & Rock Music.* Again, while
some of the claims may be correct, the implications seem to have
been insufficiently thought out.

He writes, "The rock beat places the human body under stress by increasing the pulse rate, the blood pressure, and the production of adrenaline" (p. 236). Later he adds, "Exposure to music with 'disharmonic' rhythms—whether it be the 'tension' caused by dissonance or 'noise' or the unnatural swings of misplaced rhythmical accents, syncopation, and polyrhythms, or inappropriate tempo—can result in a variety of changes including: an altered heart rate with its corresponding change in blood pressure; an overstimulation of hormones (especially the opiates or endorphins) causing an altered state of consciousness from mere exhilaration on one end of the spectrum to unconsciousness on the other; and improper digestion"[1] (p. 241).

While these physiological effects may indeed occur at times, they are effects not only of listening to rock music, but of vigorously singing hymns, of listening to marches, and of watching sports.

One might also ask, "Why is this a problem?" Speeding up the pulse is one of the goals of exercise. It's good for us, within reason.[2] The production of adrenaline is a natural phenomenon. Vigorous walking and vigorous hymn singing both lead to the release of natural opiates and endorphins. That's why one feels better after walking or singing—more relaxed, less sensitive to pain.

Dissonance can make one tense, but the organist in my church frequently uses dissonance in the hymn reharmonizations she writes. It's true that "misplaced rhythmical accents, syncopation, and polyrhythms" can make one want to hop around, but given the many references to God-approved dancing in the Scriptures,[3] this is not necessarily a problem, in its place. It is certainly not "unnatural" or unhealthy.

Sognefest writes, "Critics of rock music generally appeal to the

---

[1] Sognefest is quoting Carol and Louis Torres, *Notes on Music* (New York: 1990), p. 19. This is a 52-page book by evangelists.

[2] On page 246 Sognefest writes that after five minutes of exposure to hard rock, the pulse rate of high school students increased by seven to 12 beats per minute. By contrast, vigorous walking can easily increase the heart rate by 50 beats or more per minute. So can *lifting* hard rocks, rather than listening to hard rock.

[3] For example, Exodus 15:20; 2 Samuel 6:14, 16; Psalm 30:11; 149:3; 150:4; Ecclesiastes 3:4; Jeremiah 31:4, 13; Matthew 11:17; Luke 7:32; 15:25.

harmful physical effects of its rhythm which overshadows the melody and lyrics. They explain that good music should consist of a combination and balance of five basic elements: Melody . . . Tone color . . . Harmony . . . Rhythm . . . Tempo" (p. 240).

One is very hard-pressed to find a rock song that does not "consist of a combination and balance" of these five. If by "balance" Sognefest means an exact balance, how can one ever tell if these five are in exact balance?

How does one balance a tempo with a melody? In any piece of music—or in various passages of a single piece—some of these receive more emphasis than others. There is nothing wrong with that. If many rock songs emphasize rhythm more than melody, surely that doesn't mean they are not music.

Consider a few problem cases. Have you ever heard a solo sung a cappella? It has no harmony! Is it then not "good" music?

Gregorian chant, praised earlier in Bacchiocchi's book, turns out not to be "good" music because it attempts to avoid rhythm and so lacks "balance." Does a song stop being "good" music if it is played too slowly, unbalancing the tempo?

Surely the waltz, the march, and many other musical forms have emphatic rhythms. In the church hymnal "Onward, Christian Soldiers" is a march, while "Morning Has Broken" is a waltz.

While Bacchiocchi condemns what poets call an iambic rhythm as particularly alien to true Christian worship, Sognefest condemns the anapestic rhythm. "Particularly harmful is the rock music which employs an 'anapestic' beat, where the last beat is the loudest, such as 'da da DA.'. . . the anapestic beat, characteristic especially of rock music, is disruptive because it is the opposite of the heartbeat and thus places the normal body's rhythm under stress. This results in perceptual difficulties and manifestations of stress. In young people these manifestations may include decreased performance in school, hyperactivity and restlessness, decreased work output, more errors, and general inefficiency. In adults the symptoms include reduced decision-making capacity on the job, a nagging feeling that things just are not right, and the loss of energy for no apparent reason" (p. 245).

Sognefest goes on to cite a study showing that a man's strength is "reduced by about a third" when he listens to an anapestic beat. If this is so, then why are hard rock songs played at professional football games? So the players will be weak? No, it's because the music pumps up the players so they can play harder, less bothered by fatigue.

What is this "anapestic beat"? It's a rhythm used on rare occasions in English poetry. Here are a few examples of the anapestic beat drawn from popular hymns. Do you notice any "perceptual difficulties" or "manifestations of stress" as you read them (or sing them)?

"On a *hill* far *away* stood an *old* rugged *cross* . . .
I will *cling* to that *old* rugged cross
And ex*change* it some *day* for a *crown.*"

"Im*mor*tal, in*vis*ible *God,* only *wise.*
In *light* inaccessible *hid* from our *eyes,*
Most *blessed,* most *glor*ious, the *An*cient of *Days,*
Al*might*y, vic*tor*ious, Thy *great* Name we *praise.*"

"How *firm* a foun*da*tion, ye *saints* of the *Lord,*
Is *laid* for your *faith* in His *ex*cellent *Word!*"

"Will there *be* any *stars,* any *stars* in my *crown?*"

Strange that I usually feel stronger after singing these hymns. Perhaps it's the lyrics that strengthen me.

I think what Sognefest is talking about is a 2/4 time signature with two eighth notes followed by a quarter note, played by the drums, or the equivalent in 4/4. This is the drumbeat in the Beatles song "Magical Mystery Tour," for those who might recall it, or the Knack's 1979 hit "My Sharona." The drummer for the Rolling Stones often uses a more sophisticated version of this beat.

This drumming pattern is certainly conducive to making people want to move in some way, but that is not necessarily bad in itself, provided the movement does no harm. I often tap my foot while singing the hymns quoted above. Perhaps the anapestic rhythm makes me do that. Is that a problem?

Music by Mozart or Haydn might help relieve stress when I'm writing or grading papers (though I prefer silence), but if I were stacking a cord of firewood, a strong anapestic rhythm or a vigorous march would help me work harder than Mozart (unless it were the overture to *The Marriage of Figaro*).

Calvin M. Johansson is a professor of music at Evangel University, an organist, and an author of books on church music. He is also, unfortunately, a musical elitist championing an ideal far removed from the tastes of many churchgoers.

He seems unaware that many of his elitist complaints about rock music also apply to hymns. He writes, "The first and most obvious trait of all pop music is that it is entertaining. . . . No matter how vehemently people deny it, pop entertains. That is why it exists. . . .

"Pop's musical composition ensures that this is so. Entertainment occurs when music is crafted devoid of musical reason. Harmony, melody, rhythm, and timbre are shaped to be fun and viscerally stimulating. Without theoretical depth, pop utilizes a construction which is empty of serious musical thought. It is one-sided, costing the listener little in the way of intellectual investment" (p. 277).

It is true that popular music is, by definition, accessible to the populace, the people, and if they enjoy it and want to listen to it, it must be entertaining in some way. Of course, where one finds music not meant to entertain in some way, one finds music virtually no one wants to listen to.

If one wants to share the gospel using music as a tool, one would do well to choose music people understand and enjoy. If one wants to touch lives, more lives are touched by what is popular than by what is understood only by some musical elite.

Is the listener's "intellectual investment" a crucial aspect of music acceptable in a worship setting? Very few hymns require such an investment, though the lyrics may reveal their meaning through study.

Indeed, most "serious" music was also written to entertain. Did Mozart write primarily to instruct? Did his patrons hire him to write a new symphony so they could be educated? Did patrons flock to his operas to be instructed? I think not.

Did Bach compose his fugues to instruct worshipers in "serious musical thought"? Handel's *Messiah* richly rewards careful study, but it's *popular* because it's popular, even though it is also "serious."

Johansson writes, "Entertainment occurs when music is crafted devoid of musical reason." This is elitist and simply untrue.

On the one hand, if "musical reason" weren't entertaining, P.D.Q. Bach would lose the audience of those who can understand his musical jokes. Some of the best-reasoned compositions are among the most delightful, even to the barely initiated.

On the other hand, a good deal of popular music is crafted with great care and complexity.[4] It is true that many popular rock musicians are not well educated musically, and some rock music is primarily guitar and drum bashing. However, even that can be done with skill and by design. Those who understand such music have no difficulty distinguishing between bands with talent and bands without it.

When I see a sentence such as "Without theoretical depth, pop utilizes a construction which is empty of serious musical thought," I get nervous. Why? Because the same thing said about popular music goes for hymns.

Many of the best hymns have lyrics by talented poets, though few indeed have lyrics by what are generally considered great poets.

---

[4] Jazz is especially well known for its complex "musical reason." I might mention Dave Brubeck, Charlie Parker, Benny Goodman, and Miles Davis. However, a number of rock musicians are classically trained, and this shows in their work. For example, the band Steely Dan in the *Aja* period; Billy Joel (whose CD of piano pieces written in homage to Rachmaninoff, Chopin, and others has recently been at the top of the classical charts); Paul Simon; and the band Emerson, Lake, & Palmer (which introduced a generation of young people to classical music, including me). Others, not classically trained, have still developed very complex music, such as Joni Mitchell, Randy Newman, and Tom Waits.

The music, though delightful and satisfying to me, is also popular and seldom betrays "serious musical thought."

I get nervous because if Johansson bothers to apply his dictum to hymns, what will we sing in church? Johansson writes, "Gut-wrenching, life-changing redemption has little in common with amusement" (p. 278). That may be, but it also has little in common with "serious musical thought."

When I imagine the sort of church Johansson prefers, I picture a century-old red brick mainstream Protestant church peopled by pillars of the community who wouldn't reveal an emotion in church if they sat on a tack.

I imagine a church where worship is not a group activity, but something interior, private, not to be shared. I imagine a church people attend because it's the socially correct thing to do, even though the membership is half what it used to be.

That is to say, I imagine a dead or dying church. He writes:

"It should be obvious that to use popular music of any type in worship simply turns worship into entertainment, no matter what category, stripe, style, or subspecies of music it is. Whether rock, CCM, swing, or ragtime is used, the end result will be the same: convoluted worship, trivialization of the faith, and immaturing of the believer.

"On the other hand, great music edifies the listener. The composer invests in the work's musical traits which call the listener to reflect seriously on levels of musical content that go beyond the temporal. With emotional and intellectual balance as a result of competent craft, musical depth in great music sympathetically resonates within the heart and mind of the listener in the manner of a gestalt" (p. 278).

"Great music" may edify Johansson, but many people do not respond to it. Furthermore, to "reflect seriously on levels of musical content" is not what people should be doing in church. They should feel emotionally exposed to God. They should feel like part of one body of believers, joyous and enthusiastic and glad to be together. They should receive and embrace God's Word for them. This happens best through vigorous hymn singing, testimony, and prayer.

Certainly "great music edifies the listener," but it is also entertainment. Whether "great music" or popular music, "special music" is essentially entertainment.

"Great music" may require more skill and training than popular music, but they both entertain, and they both focus the congregation on the performer rather than on God.

When people in the congregation sing their hearts out, they sing to God and give Him glory. When they listen to a performer, they may say amen, they may applaud, but they are not glorifying God.

The problem is more severe with instrumental solos. If the music is drawn from a well-known hymn, it may call to people's minds the words of that hymn, and so lead them toward God, at least fractionally. If the music is not drawn from such a hymn, it is secular music.

Some classically trained musicians fondly imagine that if it's classical, it's suitable for the worship service. This is not true. Neither the lack of words nor the quality of the music makes it sacred.

Is it performed by a musician who wants to give the glory to God? Fine, but that doesn't mean it is leading the congregation to do the same. We worship God well, not by giving Him the best quality of music we can dig up, but by giving Him our hearts. Listening to "serious" music is not necessarily conducive of that.

What is more, "great music" may help people be introspective. It may give them an opportunity to examine themselves. But the effect of this music is sometimes to bring the pulse back to barely thumping.

I don't believe in speaking in tongues or being slain in the Spirit, but I must say that charismatics know much more about really worshiping, maintaining an emotional and spiritual connection with God and each other over time, than do the worship leaders in the churches I generally attend.[5] Perhaps that's why they often attend church because they love it, rather than because it's the thing to do.

Johansson imagines that people attend such churches because they want entertainment. I suggest that they are more likely to attend such services not because they want to be entertained, but because they want to worship and feel the Spirit active in them.

I suggest that those who want to be entertained are more likely to attend churches in which "serious music" is the norm. There they can enjoy the beauty of the music, enjoy the sermon, all in silence, without having to participate in any worship. Watching worship happen is not the same as worshiping.

Some people are edified by "great music" (I am, though that's not what I want to hear in church). But no one is *saved* by "great music," or brought to Christ by "great music," unless it is music like *The Messiah,* combining glorious music with a glorious message. Even then, to be really moved by *The Messiah,* one needs to give in to it, to let the music and the message inhabit one.

Is this a form of trance or hypnosis? Yes, it is, to some extent, but it's a holy trance. This is why I can't listen to *The Messiah* with my heart without tears. Of course, I get the same result with "God Be With You Till We Meet Again" (the original 1880 tune by W. G. Tomer, though I like Ralph Vaughan Williams's setting, too).[6]

Johansson continues, "The competence of compositional craft determines the work's integrity. Both imagination and craft are nec-

---

[5] Not all emotions are holy, of course, and there are times when one wonders just what spirit is driving some behavior in charismatic churches. In some cases the spirit seems to be granting license to excess, and that is problematic. I am praising, rather, the best of the often-noted surrender to worship in song and praise and response to the Word and the spirit of love and unity often seen. I myself am so self-conscious, alas, that I can only sit quietly and observe in such meetings.

[6] Why does that hymn move me so much? Because when I was a child the congregation sang it together every week in church to close the service, and it reminds me of those long-ago, innocent days in a little church in Alexandria, Virginia. Also, because I long to meet my loved ones again "at Jesus' feet." One reason many—like me—prefer the old familiar hymns is because they are old and familiar—they are tied together with fond memories.

essary." What he is saying is that unless you are trained as a composer, your music will lack "integrity."

"Integrity" sounds like something music offered to God should have, doesn't it? However, this is like saying that only the greatest theologians and preachers are able to bring people to Jesus. This is certainly not the case.

Indeed, some theologians have a hard time communicating on the level of the common people (though they have an important work to do).

Most people who come to Jesus are brought by family or friends: people who often know relatively little about the Bible, but know a God worth trusting.

Similarly, more people are brought to Jesus by a simple song that touches their heart—however lacking in the "competence of compositional craft"—than by anything Chopin ever wrote, much as I enjoy his music.

If the church service is about bringing people to God and keeping them there, the question should not be "Is there any room for contemporary Christian music?" but "is there any room for classical music and pipe organs?"

Here is a categorical assertion likely to surprise people who appreciate popular music. Johansson writes, "Popular music does not aspire to the highest degree of creative excellence. It is too facile, too obvious. It lacks the musical craft and imagination of great music. While some pop songs may be better than others, none rise to the level of excellence found in serious music. It may be novel, but it does not have godly creativity.

"Since pop has no musical depth (as an art music), the inevitable conclusion is that pop creativity and Godly creativity run counter to one another. This makes pop an inadequate medium for theistic witness" (p. 280).

Johansson confuses "the highest degree of creative excellence" with "godly creativity."

Is the purpose of worship to watch the trained musical elite perform with "the highest degree of creative excellence"? Is that what it means to "make a joyful noise unto the Lord"?[7] Is that what fills us with joy and leads us to praise God with all our hearts?

We need only watch the congregational reaction to such music to see that while the saints may appreciate the "creative excellence," it does not fill them with joy, reveal to them the mighty acts of God, or result in praising Christ for the salvation He has made available to us.

It may have "musical depth," but unless there are words that guide us to God, "serious music" has little if any *spiritual* depth, and so its appropriateness in the worship service is debatable.

One might even argue that its emphasis in mainline churches has had a sizable influence on their general lack of spiritual fervor.

Is popular music "an inadequate medium for theistic witness"? Most hymns are "popular music" written not by great composers exhibiting "the highest degree of creative excellence," but by less-educated composers and lyricists who love God.

It will not do to say, "Oh, those are hymns, but when I say 'popular music,' I mean rock music and things like that." One cannot fairly argue that older popular music is acceptable, but contemporary popular music is not.

I will not dig out the old argument that many hymns were derived from barroom songs,[8] because I consider it irrelevant. Popular music is by accurate definition music appreciated by the people, whether that means top 40 rock music or hymns or praise songs, and whether the venue is a barroom or a church.

Certainly its "musical depth" varies, and we can admit that it is rarely if ever at the depth of "serious music." But I would respond that "great music" is rarely an adequate "medium for theistic witness."

When was the last time Beethoven brought anyone to Christ? "Just as I Am" is not "great music," but probably millions have sung

---

[7] Encouraged in Psalms 66:1; 81:1; 95:1, 2; 98:4, 6; 100:1.

[8] Though one of the most popular hymns in my congregation these days is sung to the tune of "Danny Boy," which is still a favorite barroom ballad in Ireland.

it while giving their hearts to God. Very few of the "great composers" wrote music for evangelism. Indeed, many of them had a rather tenuous relationship with God.

Johansson writes, "The general aesthetic principle upon which pop is based is immediate gratification. . . . Little aesthetic subtlety exists in pop" (p. 281). This is true, but the same goes for hymns. If a hymn can't be spiritually appreciated unless studied, it can't do its intended work.

What Johansson writes about the musical excellence of "serious music" compared to that of "popular music" is generally true. The problem is that he assumes there is a correlation between musical excellence and spiritual depth. There isn't.

Perhaps what Johansson has done is to take the standard arguments used in music appreciation classes to convince students that classical music has excellences that make it more deserving of study than popular music and applied them to worship. I use similar arguments when I lead students through great poetry and help them appreciate its glories, but I don't argue that the most complex poetry is the most suitable for worship. In the classroom setting, rather than the worship setting, his arguments have merits. I see no problem with helping students appreciate elitist music, because such music adds richness to their lives, and appreciating it often requires training. What he has failed to notice is that the worship service is not the proper setting for such a class. Worship is inherently "popular" in a church setting, because it is something all the people are called to do.

To say that God is best praised by giving Him the best compositions written is like Cain arguing that God is best praised by giving Him the best vegetables. It is like saying that God is better praised by a Rembrandt nude than by a Harry Anderson painting of the Resurrection and Second Coming. It's like saying that God is better praised by a Henry James novel than by a conversion story in a church paper.

How hard should we have to work to understand worship music? Johansson writes, "The primitive seeks almost immediate gratification for his tendencies whether these be biological or musical. Nor can he tolerate uncertainty. And it is because distant departures from the certainty and repose of the tonic note and lengthy delays in gratification are insufferable to him that the tonal repertory of the primitive is limited, not because he can't think of other tones. It is not his mentality that is limited, it is his maturity. . . .

"The opposite corollary of immediate gratification is delayed gratification. It is one of the key aesthetic principles employed in creating music of integrity and worth. My experience over a lifetime of rehearsing college and church choirs has been that music of delayed gratification wears well over weeks and months of rehearsal. But popular music of whatever ilk does not fare as well. Choristers tire of rehearsing its predictable tunes and harmonies" (pp. 281-283).

This may well be true,[9] but the fact is that it's hard to find a great hymn that doesn't return to the tonic, to "certainty and repose," within eight bars. They all get back home by the end of the verse and chorus, which means a delay of no more than about 20 seconds.

It may well be true that singing hymns bores choirs addicted to "music of integrity and worth," but such choirs singing such worthwhile music rarely have an evangelistic impact. The purpose of hymns is to have an immediate impact, not to engage listeners with complex music that delays their gratification.

Enjoying "great music" is so pleasurable that I think everyone should be taught how, but it is a *learned* ability requiring a good deal of musical sophistication.

We can no more expect seekers to come to us with such abilities than we can expect them to be able to find the various books of the Bible when they first pick one up. People can be trained to enjoy this music, but the worship service is not the place to do it, and if

---

[9] Though to be fair we might point out that the "primitive" drum polyrhythms of Africa sometimes take 10 minutes or more before they come together and the rhythmic scheme can be comprehended. The Grateful Dead were famous for using a similar approach to their songs, sometimes keeping the audience in suspense for 20 minutes before the instruments gradually came together.

we play this music in church, we are catering to the elite.[10]

Johansson writes, "Gut-wrenching, life-changing redemption has little in common with amusement" (p. 278). It has even less in common with "serious music."

He writes that popular music "is unable to display general revelatory gospel witness. Pop music simply has little in common with the gospel" (p. 284). Frankly, I can't figure out how he could come to such a conclusion if he had the slightest familiarity with popular Christian music.

For example, Thomas Dorsey composed jazz and blues songs before he turned to gospel, and that background is always evident in his music. His song "Precious Lord, Take My Hand" is still a favorite of jazz and soul singers and instrumentalists. But Dorsey's life was dedicated to "gospel witness," and that song reveals in essence the correct stance for the repentant sinner, as described by Jesus (Luke 18:13). It reveals it even in smoky nightclubs, where it is still sometimes played.

Again, Johansson writes, "Music of artistry assumes the normalcy of high expectations. Composers don't write 'down' to an audience, even at the subconscious level. Unlike pop composition, which exists within an assumed framework of the necessity of mass acceptability, art music expects the listener to rise to the standard set by art work" (p. 284). Thus such music doesn't reach most people. By definition, this *limits* its use as a vehicle of the gospel.

He writes, "Grace calls us to a higher standard than the law ever did" (p. 285). This is true, but it doesn't call us to a higher *musical* standard. We are not *saved* by "art songs." Salvation does not depend on appreciation of "serious music."

Johansson writes, "No composer worth his salt would allow his musical integrity to be compromised by strictures to his composi-

---

[10] When I was in college I attended a local Unitarian church a number of times as part of a class assignment. What I noticed was that the music was always superb, catering to the intellectual elite, and the sermons were also intellectually satisfying, but didn't mention the Bible. Bible teaching and "art music" don't really go together very well.

tional technique. The making of a genuine work of art is not tied to acceptability" (p. 288). Surely Mozart and Bach, among many others, often had to write what they were told to write.

If "a work of art" isn't accessible to the audience, reviews are bad, people don't come to performances, and commissions dry up. Verdi, Puccini, and Gilbert and Sullivan were all under intense pressure to produce "hits." Even Handel wrote *The Messiah* hoping it would be a hit.

Johansson complains, "Thus, churches have to pay a royalty to use most CCM. . . . Although the gospel is inherently noncommercial, commercialism shapes the church's worship when religious pop music is used" (p. 289).

What he neglects to mention—though as a choir director he surely knows it—is that churches have to pay to use "serious music" under copyright too, or at least spend hundreds of dollars for choir parts, which has the same effect. Dare we mention that many ministers of music and soloists also expect to be paid?

The chapter by Günter Preuss is titled "Rock Music and Evangelism." Preuss is a church music director who was finishing his dissertation on "reformed hymnody between 1700 and 1870" at the Sorbonne when he contributed this article.[11]

What is the difference between "sacred" and "secular" music? Preuss writes, "There are those who contend that music per se is neither sacred or secular—it is a neutral thing. For them, what makes music 'sacred' is not its style, but its lyrics. This popular view is flawed

---

[11] After this book was accepted for publication, I had the privilege of spending several pleasant hours with Preuss while on a speaking tour in Germany. I found him to be a thoughtful, reasonable, tolerant man who is not only a highly trained scholar, but a jazz pianist who enthusiastically leads song services of praise songs, even though that is not his favorite music, and is popular with young people. By the end of our discussion he had decided that he was relatively comfortable with all of the personal and congregational guidelines I've suggested in this book, except that he withheld judgment regarding the relative moral neutrality of music apart from lyrics until he had studied my ideas more carefully. If I disagree with several of his assertions in the pages that follow, please understand that I am merely disagreeing with a few statements made by a friend, and that his comments primarily work as springboards for my own thinking.

both historically, theologically, and scientifically" (p. 303). He continues, "Sanctification presupposes a separation from the world in order to be set aside and consecrated to the service of God. Whatever is used for the service of God is sacred, that is, set aside for holy use. This is true not only of music but of speech as well. The profane language used in the street is inappropriate in church. In the same way, rock music used in bars or nightclubs to stimulate people physically cannot be used in the church to elevate people spiritually" (p. 303).

I don't know about Preuss, but I speak the same language "in the street" that I speak in church: English. One gets the idea he'd prefer a return to a Latin liturgy (though this is not in fact the case), but that too was a street language when it entered the church.

Certainly there are words I *hear* in the street that are not appropriate in church, but of course they aren't appropriate in the street, either, and I don't use such language. Also, I don't hesitate to speak about God in the street (or in my classroom in a secular university). I know a few people who talk about God only in church, but I question their Christian commitment.

It's true that "sanctification presupposes a separation from the world," but only in a manner of speaking, and not in the way he claims.

I cannot say that I've ever heard in church "rock music heard in bars," unless the song had Christian lyrics (and rock songs with Christian lyrics are occasionally heard in bars).

On the other hand, I've often heard in church the compositions of Chopin or Debussy, and I'm not aware that these compositions are considered sacred. They are certainly much heard in the secular concert hall.

Even the work of Bach, who understood himself to be writing to the glory of God, is not inherently sacred. If we see his fugues as sacred, it is only because we've heard some of them in church. I'm fond of "Jesu, Joy of Man's Desiring," but I don't know any other words from the song, and without those words I'd have no way of knowing the song was to be considered sacred.

The psalms sung in the Temple services were available for anyone to sing while plowing a field. Today our bodies are temples of the Holy Ghost. This suggests that we should avoid defiling them with what is impure—including music—but it also means there is no difference between what is appropriate music for Christians in church and what is appropriate for Christians anywhere else, except that when Christians worship together, they should avoid music that offends some who are present.

Are some types of singing more appropriate in the worship service? Preuss writes, "Rock singing does not use the techniques of classical music based on a relaxed larynx and rich harmonic overtones. Instead, it employs high-pitched strained voicing" (p. 304). This is not strictly true.

Many of the top R&B singers use these classical techniques. These techniques were perfected in and for the opera, but opera is far from sacred. The techniques are beautiful to those who have learned to appreciate them, but they are artificial (that is, they are achieved through artifice, through the mastery of an art). They help singers achieve volume and control and protect their voices, but that doesn't make them holy.

Indeed, the very artificiality of the operatic voice may lessen its effectiveness in evangelistic witness, even with an inherently evangelistic song, because the vocal style is so beautiful, so focused on the production of the perfect sound, that it can seem insincere.

There's more sincerity and authenticity in the cracked and scratchy voice of an out-of-tune old saint humbly singing God's praises than in the glorious voices of Placido Domingo or Leontyne Price.

Of course, most hymn-singers don't use these techniques either. When it comes down to it, we aren't saved by "relaxed larynxes," and "rich harmonic overtones" bring few people to God.[12]

---

[12] I might also mention that the "high-pitched strained voicing" of many popular singers is just as deliberate as the operatic voice of Luciano Pavarotti, though less trained. The best of these popular singers have very distinctive, recognizable voices admired and praised by those trained to appreciate them. Most aspiring popular singers fail to develop such a voice. Just as one can learn to appreciate the forms of excellence in the operatic voice, one can learn to appreciate the varied forms of excellence found in popular singing.

Preuss writes, "Musically speaking, most 'Christian' rock is no different from secular rock, except for the lyrics" (p. 306). Musically speaking, Verdi's *Requiem* isn't much different from his opera *La Traviata,* either, except for the lyrics, but we know better, I would hope, than to perform the latter in church.

What is "vain repetition"? Preuss writes, "Two major problems with CWM [contemporary worship music] is that it generally incorporates rock rhythms with a heavy bass line and is very repetitious. Jesus warned against using vain repetitions in worship (Matt. 6:7)" (p. 306). This is not, of course, what Jesus meant by "Do not use vain repetitions as the heathen do" (NKJV).

What about the four living creatures of Revelation 4, who "never stop saying: 'Holy, holy, holy is the Lord God Almighty, who was, and is, and is to come'" (verse 8, NIV)? Repetition is not *vain* unless it is *in vain.* When the heathen pray to gods of wood and stone, they are not heard—their prayers are in vain. They repeat their prayers over and over because they think this will help their gods hear them.[13]

That's not why we repeat the Lord's Prayer year after year. We may ask God many times for something, such as healing or safety, but that is not "vain repetition." We may say "Lord" or "Father" many times in our prayers, but that's not "vain repetition" either, even though it may be so redundant as to sound more like a hiccup than a consciously called-on name.

We sing many hymns that repeat words or phrases in choruses, such as "When the Roll Is Called Up Yonder."[14] What about "Praise Him, Praise Him!"? Is that too repetitive? What about "So Send I You" or "Amazing Grace" or "Lift Up the Trumpet"?

---

[13] By contrast, when Roman Catholics say the rosary, it is not because repetition makes it more likely God will hear them, but because it both focuses the mind on God and clears the mind of the detritus of worldly worries, making it easier for God's voice to be heard.

[14] That was a favorite hymn of mine when I was a child, because of the bouncy beat, but I thought the phrase was "When the road is called a pyonder," and I often wondered why it would be called that.

By condemning contemporary worship music Preuss implicitly condemns many of the favorite hymns of our past.[15] It is true that when praise songs are sung in charismatic churches, they are often repeated several times, and this can have an emotional effect on audiences, but these emotions are holy.

May God forbid that we try to keep the people of God from praising him over and over as best they know how. The first praise song known to have been written in English is also the oldest surviving English poem, "Caedmon's Hymn." It was composed by an illiterate herdsman and preserved for us by the greatest theologian of his day, Bede.[16]

Preuss writes, "Christian rock artists, stemming from different churches, espouse virtually the same expression of a minimal Gospel. Doctrinal differences do not really matter and should not be expressed in song. What matters is joining together in praising the Lord. . . .

"Evangelistic music, instead of bringing people from the world to Christ, often brings the world's agenda into the church, thus undermining the identity and mission of the church (p. 308)."

You might note that your own church's hymnal has relatively few hymns dealing with denominational doctrinal distinctives.

Indeed, most were written by Christians of other denominations. Some were revised to remove doctrinal ideas we do not accept. Hymns cross denominational lines quite easily. For example, the

---

[15] Though, as I've written above, Preuss is a very talented song leader, even when singing praise songs, and as the author of a 3,500-page dissertation on hymns, he is an expert on the topic.

[16] Bede writes of Caedmon, in *An Ecclesiastical History of the English People* (c. 731), "It often happened that his songs kindled a contempt for this world and a longing for the life of Heaven in the hearts of many men. Indeed, after him others among the English people tried to compose religious poetry, but no one could equal him because he was not taught the art of song by men or by human agency but received this gift through heavenly grace. Therefore, he was never able to compose any vain and idle songs but only such as dealt with religion and were proper for his religious tongue to utter" (*The Norton Anthology of English Literature: The Middle Ages,* seventh ed. [New York: Norton, 2000], p. 24). Note that these were popular songs, composed and sung by an untrained man.

song "Majesty," a praise song often sung in the church I attend, was written by a leading charismatic pastor, Jack Hayford.

There is a big difference between bringing "the world's agenda into the church" and using songs written by Christians from other denominations. It is, rather, "serious music" that brings in the world's way of judging quality and places "art" above popular congregational appeal.

Conclusion

Though I have not discussed the final three chapters of *The Christian & Rock Music,* I think I've made my point sharply enough. There are some good things about the book. Osterman makes some good points, though her comments about various types of African-American music and some of their characteristics seem unfair, and some of her arguments are simplistic. Stefani's chapter is not objectionable, and he has more reputable sources than the other authors. I was drawn to Brian Neumann's personal testimony as a person who has actually been a successful rock musician but given it up.

I agree with all of the writers that rock music with secular lyrics poses real dangers for Christian young people, easily turning their focus away from God. Trying to stay close to God while listening to a lot of secular rock music is a bit like trying to remain a virgin while sharing a bed with your boyfriend. It can be done, but it makes life a lot more difficult.

There are several places where the book fails. It fails to realize the serious difference between CCM and secular popular music. If the authors had spent a few days reading the lyrics of CCM songs and reading interviews with CCM musicians, I think the book might have been much different.

There are certainly problems with a lot of secular music and the musicians who perform it. That does not mean it is fair to also tar Christian musicians whose music may sound similar, though the words and philosophy are wildly different.

Similarly, there are problems with a lot of secular *people.* Does that mean all secular people should be avoided? Does it mean Christian people should be avoided, since they too are people?

There are young people with wild hair and clothes and tattoos and body piercings who make appallingly bad choices. I've also had students who look like that who are seeking God. We must judge a tree according to its fruit, not its leaves.

The book fails because the authors fail to notice that CCM of all sorts has a huge positive influence on listeners. Most of the musicians I've read about seem to see themselves primarily as missionaries. That doesn't mean they are necessarily seeing conversions and baptisms, but many are.

In some cases their lyrics are quite elliptical, and it takes a good deal of thought to recognize the religious content.[17] Sometimes this is because the musicians are trying to reach out to people who have an antipathy to Christian triumphalism. At other times it is because they see themselves as musicians who are Christians, rather than as Christian musicians. In this case the lyrics reflect the questions and struggles of the Christian heart in a truthful way.

We can't all always be bubbling over with Jesus' love, and sometimes we need to know that others face the same problems.

The book fails because its "research" is based primarily on sensationalistic sources and on the work of other writers who haven't thought out the implications of their arguments and whose claims are inaccurate and based on literalistic readings of their sources.

The writers seldom turn to primary research by scientists publishing in scholarly journals for their information on the physiological effect of music, for example. Also, nearly all the bad examples are drawn from the most notorious secular rock musicians.

This may help us understand the ideal relationship between the Christian and secular rock music, but it doesn't help us understand the ideal relationship between the Christian and contemporary

---

[17] Just as Johansson argues that "serious music" doesn't reveal itself all at once, the same is true with serious poetry and lyrics. There is a place for Christian lyrics that take some work.

Christian music. If there is a difference, and there is, it should be acknowledged.

The book fails because of its shocking lack of tolerance of differences in taste. As I read the book, with a couple exceptions, what I sensed over and over is that what these authors consider acceptable music for everyone is the music they themselves like, and what they consider unacceptable music is the music they don't like.

I myself don't listen to CCM by choice, but I do listen to it with my sons when they ask me to, and I judge it according to what it is and is trying to do, not according to whether or not I like it. I try to judge the music according to its fruits. How does it make people behave? Does it lead them to sin? Does it lead them to Christ?

Experience proves beyond doubt that contemporary Christian music in its many forms is leading many listeners to a closer walk with God.

Finally, the book fails because time after time its biblical support is based on eisegesis rather than exegesis. I've seldom seen in one book so many weak interpretations and so few sound ones.

The subtitle of the book is "A Study on Biblical Principles of Music." Frankly, the Bible says virtually nothing specifically about music that helps us determine biblical principles. There are two texts that give us principles we can use.

One is Philippians 4:8: "Finally, brethren, whatsoever things are true, whatsoever things are honest, whatsoever things are just, whatsoever things are pure, whatsoever things are lovely, whatsoever things are of good report; if there be any virtue, and if there be any praise, think on these things."

The other is Colossians 3:16: "Let the word of Christ dwell in you richly in all wisdom; teaching and admonishing one another in psalms and hymns and spiritual songs, singing with grace in your hearts to the Lord." Whatever combination of words and music meets those criteria is fine for praising God, whether or not you or I like it.

That doesn't mean it's necessarily appropriate in church, where there is a need for unity and there may be many people who don't like it, but it's appropriate for those who like it, whether they be alone or in a group.[18]

Also, if any combination of words and music that meets these criteria proves itself able to touch the hearts of unbelievers, it is fine for evangelistic purposes, even though it might not be appropriate in an actual evangelistic campaign with a wide range of people attending.

These authors are my brothers and sisters in Christ, and some are friends. If the book were not selling well, if it were not having an influence on pastors and church members, I would not devote my energy to exposing its weaknesses. However, because it is in fact having a large influence, I provide this so others can refer to it as necessary.

As I've said, the fate of our young people is far too important to allow the influence of one ill-considered book to turn them away from God. They need our friendship and counsel, and they want it. We need to know the right things to say and the right way to say them.

---

[18] Hayden writes, "True worship can happen only as a congregation is unified in both spirit and truth. Anything that interrupts this unity will destroy the heavenly atmosphere of worship. Thus it is vital that as worshipers we bring to the sanctuary not only a reverent attitude toward God, but a Christlike spirit toward those with whom we worship. Once again it means that we be sensitive to those things that might offend others—in this case, music" (Hayden, *Lifestyles of the Remnant,* pp. 81, 82).

Chapter 7

Why We Need
Contemporary Christian Music

I do not sit with the worthless,
nor do I consort with hypocrites;
I hate the company of evildoers,
and will not sit with the wicked.
I wash my hands in innocence,
and go around your altar, O Lord,
singing aloud a song of thanksgiving,
and telling all your wondrous deeds.
—Psalm 26:4-7, NRSV

Two of the most intelligent books written about CCM are Charlie Peacock's *At the Crossroads: An Insider's Look at the Past, Present, and Future of Contemporary Christian Music* and Mark Joseph's *The Rock & Roll Rebellion: Why People of Faith Abandoned Rock Music—And Why They're Coming Back.*[*]

Charlie Peacock is a well-known musician, composer, and producer. At the Crossroads is written primarily for CCM artists who know what the industry is like, rather than presenting "An Insider's Look" for those who are not inside. The book is rather like a series of worship talks for musicians on the importance of surrender and transformation and letting God use them as fully as possible. For some musicians, this might come as news. For others, it might recall them to their mission.

Peacock's primary intent is to convince musicians to leave the

---

[*] Both Nashville: Broadman & Holman, 1999.

somewhat cloistered world of CCM and go out into the world to spread the gospel, rather than continually preaching to the choir.

Joseph's book reads like a series of case studies in support of Peacock's book. Joseph presents insightful spiritual and musical biographies of dozens of musicians. Some became rock stars, then accepted Christ and gave up their careers in the secular music world, preferring the smaller world of CCM or giving up music altogether. Some did this, then returned to the mainstream. Others began in CCM, then broke into the mainstream, or tried.

Both Peacock and Joseph claim the late Bob Briner's book *Roaring Lambs* as a major influence. Briner's contention is that the reason one doesn't see or hear more Christians in the mass media—television, music, movies, newspapers—is that they've withdrawn from the world. He argues that Christian performers need to take over the media for Christ by establishing a presence there.

This is a bit like missionaries establishing an outpost in some benighted land, and it's a worthy aim. However, just as missionaries in some Muslim countries must be extremely circumspect or risk a violent death, Christian musicians in the mainstream who wear their faith on their sleeve and make altar calls at concerts risk either a swift end to their career or a lingering but terminal loss of influence.

Briner seems to think that merely having Christians in high places is a good thing. It's true that we are called to be salt, seasoning the world, but, as Jesus said, "If the salt have lost his savour, wherewith shall it be salted?" (Matt. 5:13). Some Christian musicians provide so little Christian flavor to their work that it's hard to know they're Christians. As Jesus points out, they, the salt, need to be salted, but one shouldn't need to salt the salt before it tastes salty.

Joseph inadvertently provides examples of this. Most people who have listened to rock music over the past 30 years have heard of the groups Peter, Paul, and Mary, Poco, Santana, Wings, Grand Funk Railroad, Kansas, U2, Run-D.M.C., and Van Halen, but how many realized that all of these included at least one Christian? I had no idea! Perhaps this is because the Christians had to be very quiet if they wanted to keep on selling records.

Several Christian bands, such as dc Talk, Audio Adrenaline, MxPx, Jars of Clay, and P.O.D., have had a good deal of success in the secular music world, and their songs are even found on movie sound tracks and played during televised sports events. But how is this possible?

It comes down to lyrics. Sometimes the lyrics are mixed down so far that they can barely be heard. More often they are so subtle, so allusive, that they might better be called cryptic. As a poetry teacher, I am of course a fan of subtle lyrics. I have to admit, though, that probably few listeners realize they are listening to a Christian message.

It's possible, of course, that many people hear and like the songs, not knowing what they mean, then buy the CD, then as they listen over and over are gradually exposed to the gospel. Indeed, I suspect that often happens.

One of the bravest of all Christian converts is Bob Dylan, who nearly ruined his career by recording several overtly Christian albums in which nearly every song challenged listeners to accept Christ. I have great respect for Dylan. However, for the past 15 years his recordings have been more circumspect. When I read the lyrics, I see that he is still a Christian, but he's learned to be "wise as serpents, and harmless as doves" (Matt. 10:16), so much so that some critics don't realize he's still a Christian. As he seems no longer to be a threat, he is once again popular, once again winning awards and selling millions of CDs.

It's paradoxical that the hotter musicians are to share Christ, the more they turn off the general audience. It's possible to consider oneself a Christian without one's audience realizing it, but then one has little influence.

Most people are receptive to songs about a spiritual search, so long as nothing too exciting is found. They're receptive to songs that lead them to question where they are and what they believe, so long as no alternative is thrust down their throat.

The problem is that the sorts of musicians who themselves write such songs tend to be searchers themselves. If born-again Christians sing about how they're searching for an answer, in order to reach those who are also searching, when actually they've already found the answer, then they're not being strictly honest, and they risk people's turning cynical if they find out.

There are also well-known Christian artists, such as Amy Grant, who have gone mainstream with some success. However, they've usually found that they are pressured to record more non-religious songs (though Grant's latest album is a collection of hymns).

Both Peacock and Joseph ask with rightful irritation why every song a Christian musician writes or records should deal in some way with God. Isn't there a need for, say, songs by Christians about love, social problems, family, or other aspects of life? Certainly there is. The problem is that the Christian witness becomes less obvious. This isn't necessarily bad, but it's there.

If we are God's representatives, then whatever subject we deal with in lyrics needs to be from God's point of view, or we are not accurately representing Him as His ambassadors. If we are God's stewards, then our lyrics should aim at preserving (saving) His creation.

There are many ways of doing this in lyrics, many levels of "God-talk" one might fairly use. But this doesn't mean Christian musicians can write about whatever they want, as if the important thing were simply to have a lot of Christian musicians, so all the musicians won't be non-Christians.

Not only is it not easy to make it in the mainstream music world, but there are several dangers for Christian musicians. First, it's quite possible for Christians to listen exclusively to Christian music, but Christian musicians seldom have this luxury. They need to know what their non-Christian peers are doing. As they listen, they risk being influenced not only by the music but by the lyrics. (Similarly, as an English professor I can choose to teach only literature I think would be pleasing in God's eyes, but I have to study a much wider range myself, so that I have more perspective.)

Second, there is a big difference between performing for

Christian audiences and performing for general audiences. There are much bigger temptations, and it is much easier to slip and fall. Christian musicians outside the world of CCM need to pay special attention to their walk with God, and the wise ones find mentors who can help them remain faithful. As contractors tell me, it's hard enough to walk straight on the ground, but it's even harder, yet more important, when you are walking on top of a two-by-four stud wall eight feet above the ground. Perfect balance and fast reflexes are a requirement for both occupations.

If musicians are making altar calls or preaching Christ at a concert, the audience knows where they are coming from, even if the audience rejects that, and the drug pushers and groupies are more likely to keep their distance. When musicians are praying with kids after a concert, there's a lot less temptation. But when musicians are Christians but keeping it quiet at a concert, the temptation is much worse. Will anyone see me? Who will know? You might say it's like the difference between being a guerrilla and being a mole. The guerilla (the overt Christian musician at the CCM concert) gets the excitement and the combat, but the spy (the covert Christian at the mainstream concert) gets the stress.

Third, when musicians move from CCM to mainstream music, they often take fans with them—indeed, they wouldn't want to leave their entire following behind and start over. However, by doing so, they are exposing their fans not only to their own music but to the rest of the music out there. Young people who listened only to Christian music may now begin listening to everything. Much of what they hear will make it harder to remain connected to God. Musicians need to bear in mind that they will bear some of the responsibility for this.

So Why Does CCM Matter?

I've read interviews with CCM artists who keep lists of how many people are "saved" at their concerts. Peacock tells us that they are even under pressure from concert promoters to make altar calls and show results. It is, of course, difficult to get statistics on how many young people are "saved" at a concert. It's even harder to find out how many remain "saved" the next morning or week or year. Pity the poor band that performs to a sold-out crowd of Christians with not a sinner among them!

Promoters who gauge musical success by the number of "Commitment to Christ" cards turned in at the end of a show, however, are missing something more important. As Peacock writes, a one-time commitment that isn't followed by discipling will not yield a true Christian. However, that's not all.

The fact is, very few people accept Christ the first time they are presented with the gospel. Many hear it a thousand times before they are finally willing to submit to it, and life suddenly seems very different.

At a CCM concert where most of the kids would call themselves Christians, a large percentage have not yet truly submitted to God and don't yet have evidence in their lives of being born again, even though they may consider themselves born again. The concert may be the "straw that breaks the camel's back," but more likely it will lead kids one step closer to surrender.

Then too, there is sanctification to be considered. Even after we truly surrender to God and accept salvation, we still have a lot of growing to do. It may be that at a CCM concert, a number of those "already Christian" kids will come one step closer to where God wants them to be.

Is this a small thing, a minor improvement? Just ask their parents. Maybe it's something someone says. Maybe it's some mysterious connection made in their minds as they're praying. Maybe it's just the way someone's guitar sounds. A song that moves one person in a wonderful way because that one person has just the right spiritual need may not touch anyone else in the audience that night.

I would suggest to those who, like Peacock and Joseph, downplay the importance of CCM in light of the need to reach out to the world, that CCM performs an extremely useful function in gradually leading believers closer to God.

In the audience there may be no two people at the same place on the path, yet it may be that everyone on that path is led up a bit higher. So even if not one person at a concert makes "a decision for Christ" for the first time, it may be that hundreds of people are reconfirming their decisions for Christ in their hearts. That's important!

There's no need for musicians to be apologetic about playing CCM concerts. If we learned everything we need to know when we accepted Christ, why do we need preachers? Why do I spend most of my time studying the Word, always discovering new things, and teaching those things? There's nothing I want more for my children than for them to have eternal life, and if CCM helps them persevere and grow in Christ, I am grateful.

Also, there's a need to *maintain faith*. All of us have periods when we're farther from God than we were before, periods of discouragement, doubt, or depression. At a CCM concert, listeners in unity with many other listeners may rediscover the excitement of life in the Spirit. They may come away recharged for the fight against evil. That's very important!

If a CCM band never brought a single person to Christ for the first time, but helped many people persevere who might otherwise have turned to a life of sin, it could look forward to hearing Christ say "Well done."

Here's another way CCM serves a valuable purpose. Songs, whatever they are, fill the head and the heart. Songs of ugliness, crime, and sin fill the mind and heart with ugliness, crime, and sin. Songs of goodness and God fill the mind and heart with goodness and God.

It's harder for Satan to tempt us when we have Christian songs in our heads. Often when I'm tempted in some way, I'll whistle a hymn, and the temptation drops away. Thus CCM keeps us away from evil, preserves us. We are told to think on what is good and true. CCM helps believers do that. No need to apologize.

Chapter 8

Joyful Worship

I ask not only on behalf of these, but also on behalf of those who will believe in me through their word, *that they may all be one.* As you, Father, are in me and I am in you, *may they also be in us, so that the world may believe that you have sent me.* The glory that you have given me I have given them, *so that they may be one,* as we are one, I in them and you in me, *that they may become completely one, so that the world may know that you have sent me* and have loved them even as you have loved me.
—John 17:20-23, NRSV.

Let the word of Christ dwell in you richly; *teach and admonish one another* in all wisdom; and with gratitude in your hearts *sing psalms, hymns, and spiritual songs to God.*
—Colossians 3:16, NRSV

Be filled with the Spirit, as you *sing psalms and hymns and spiritual songs among yourselves,* singing and making melody to the Lord in your hearts, *giving thanks* to God the Father at all times and for everything in the name of our Lord Jesus Christ.
—Ephesians 5:18-20, NRSV

What should be done then, my friends? When you come together, each one has a hymn, a lesson, a revelation, a tongue, or an interpretation. Let all things be done for building up.
—1 Corinthians 14:26, NRSV

How might we go about incorporating the ideas I've shared in this book in a worship service? In this chapter I will propose an order of service that would help build a feeling of unity in a congregation, then give my rationale for the changes I've made from the more traditional way of doing things. Bear in mind that the traditional approach is not a law of God, but merely a tradition of human beings. Is this approach hallowed by tradition? Tradition hallows nothing.

On the other hand, tradition is not necessarily bad. My sister is an active member of a very traditional African-American church, and when she read the manuscript of this book she was upset. She doesn't want her church to change! I won't deny that there are plenty of churches that are traditional in form yet filled with love, unity, and heartfelt worship. If that is the case, may God bless them. They're doing something right, and they don't need to change.

The problem is that most congregations I've worshiped with that follow traditions formed in past generations are lukewarm or dead, whether large or small. When traditions are followed because "That's the way it's always been done," rather than because they resonate in the heart, they have lost their power. It is sometimes possible to resurrect dead traditions by helping believers recover their first love, helping them understand the precious connotations of the traditions, but this isn't easy.

It's much easier to start new traditions that seem meaningful to a new generation. Because these old traditions are the traditions of individuals, not the commands of God, they are not sacred, even though they occur in a sacred service. That means we are free to substitute something that works.

What follows is not the only way to resurrect a dying church, but it's one way. It's a sort of shock therapy to awaken and reset minds that have strayed into unproductive channels. Used in the wrong way—with closed hearts—it can become an enjoyable substitute for true worship. If it leads people to open their hearts to one another and to God, though, then it can be a wonderful experience.

Where I worship, we have followed a traditional order of service for many years. A few years ago we began prefacing it with a healthy period of singing and testimony. As people sing and testify, they begin opening to each other and to God. However, the order of worship we follow suggests that this is not a true part of the worship service, but a prelude to it. The "real" worship service begins when the pastor and elders walk onto the platform and kneel in prayer. Then the Doxology is sung, there is an invocation and welcome, and an opening hymn accompanied by the organ.

As in many churches these days, we then collect a "lamb's offering"—the smaller children walk around collecting money for our church building project—and have a children's story. Then the regular offering is collected as the organ plays. There is "special music," a few verses of Scripture are read, and there is a prayer. Then the pastor speaks. After he has finished, there is a closing hymn, a benediction, and an organ postlude as we are dismissed by rows. By the time the last worshipers exit, some of those who sat in the front of the church are already driving home.

The problem with this traditional order of service is that any fervor built up during the song service dissipates during what follows, because apart from the hymns, the congregants are spectators rather than participators. By the time the pastor begins to speak, the congregation is already growing drowsy, reading the Bible or a church magazine, or planning lunch or the afternoon's activities. Thus they don't always learn what the pastor wants to teach, or remember even ten minutes later what he said. It's no wonder that the pastor is sometimes so frustrated by this passivity as to call out, "Is anybody out there?"

There are some denominations that emphasize quiet introspection rather than building congregational unity. Worshipers are meant to search their souls, forget about those sitting around them, and enter into a private reverie. Periods of meditation while the organ plays quietly and instrumental performances help establish this mood. While introspection is a good thing in private worship, quiet meditation has no New Testament support in congregational worship. The "Let All Mortal Flesh Keep Silence" approach to worship is partly responsible for an alarming decrease in membership in many of these denominations.

118

Some readers may feel that reverent introspection is the only appropriate way to worship or believe that a hearty "Amen" is out of place during a sermon or after a testimony. I find the following advice on this matter helpful:

"Praise the Lord in the congregation of His people. When the word of the Lord was spoken to the Hebrews anciently, the command was: 'And let all the people say, Amen.' When the ark of the covenant was brought into the city of David, and a psalm of joy and triumph was chanted, 'all the people said, Amen, and praised the Lord.' *This fervent response was an evidence that they understood the word spoken and joined in the worship of God.*

"*There is too much formality in our religious services.* The Lord would have His ministers who preach the Word energized by His Holy Spirit; and *the people who hear should not sit in drowsy indifference, or stare vacantly about, making no responses to what is said.* The impression that is thus given to the unbeliever is anything but favorable for the religion of Christ. These dull, careless professed Christians are not destitute of ambition and zeal when engaged in worldly business; but things of eternal importance do not move them deeply. The voice of God through His messengers may be a pleasant song; but its sacred warnings, reproofs, and encouragements are all unheeded. The spirit of the world has paralyzed them. The truths of God's Word are spoken to leaden ears and hard, unimpressible hearts. There should be wide-awake, active churches to encourage and uphold the ministers of Christ and to aid them in the work of saving souls. *Where the church is walking in the light, there will ever be cheerful, hearty responses and words of joyful praise*" (Ellen G. White, *Testimonies for the Church,* vol. 5, p. 318; italics supplied).

If this is correct, then most churches I attend are not walking in the light. They are too drowsy and too indifferent to God's message to them.

Athletes play better when fans cheer them on. A comedy routine can be destroyed if the audience doesn't laugh. Secular musicians are not spurred on to greater efforts by a smattering of applause.

I'm not suggesting that pastors are primarily performers or should try to make the congregation laugh, but in a way preaching is a lot like walking a tightrope: it's scary, it requires careful balance, and one is often merely one false step from disaster. Congregational response is a great help.

I've sometimes preached the same sermon to three congregations in one day, with wildly different results. When people respond with amens, I feel strengthened and encouraged. When they sit silently, even if they are listening intently, I begin to feel panic and desperation seeping into my mind. Aren't people listening? Do they disagree with me? Am I not communicating what I've been given to share?

If you want an interesting pastor, a good place to start is to arrange with a group of friends to lift the person up with amens. I'm not talking about frivolity, but about noticing true statements when they occur, things you agree with, and affirming them with your voice. You may be surprised by how fast your pastor's speaking improves.

The proposals that follow are meant to deal with problems caused by traditions that have lost their meaning and offer a more rational and more biblical approach that will build unity. Nearly everything before the sermon in this order of worship is participatory. This allows enough time to build fervor and open hearts before the sermon.

Why, some might ask, do we need this fervor to open our hearts? Some of us already have open hearts as we sit reverently with our hands folded and our heads bowed. This may well be, but congregational worship should be about worshiping together, not worshiping individually in the same room.

Consider this analogy drawn from the world of exercise. Some people are so athletic that their cardiovascular systems are always in excellent condition. Most of us, however, benefit from regular aerobic activities, such as vigorous walking. Researchers have found that aerobic exercise has little effect on the condition of one's heart unless the heartbeat reaches a certain minimum rate and the rate is maintained for quite a while. Walking for five minutes, then resting for five minutes, is not aerobic activity for most people.

Similarly, opening the heart to God and to others in congregational worship is not automatic for most of us. We need to maintain the spiritual exercise that leads to openness until the desired effect occurs. If we stop to rest for five minutes while the offering is collected, we have to start all over. All of the recommendations below are meant to open and strengthen our hearts.

Three Useful Approaches to Worship

Here are three ways of looking at congregational worship. The first uses a "king and subjects" metaphor. This is the dominant Old Testament view of worship. God's presence dwells in a sanctuary. God's people approach Him, but dare not get too close, lest they be consumed. This may be the root of the original meaning of the English word "worship"—ascribing "worth-ship" to someone.

Imagine the worship service as a group of citizens coming to a palace to meet with their king. When they enter and see him on his throne, they spend a long time praising him, in song and testimony, for what he has done for them. They quote some of his promises to them. They ask him for help. Then, having listened, the king responds to his citizens, both through the reading of what he has written to them and through the one who speaks for him. He teaches and admonishes them. The citizens respond to the king with thanks, then return to their homes.

The traditional model of worship is similar to this, and the suggestions that follow are based on it. However, we need to bear in mind that this is not the only metaphor for the relationship between God and his people.

The Bible also teaches that this relationship is like that between a bride and a bridegroom or a husband and a wife. God is the bridegroom and His people are His wife. If a bride looks bored or unhappy at her wedding reception, her bridegroom will be disappointed. If my wife decides to show me "reverence" by bowing before me, her forehead to the floor, and humbly waiting for me to speak words of wisdom, I won't be pleased. Our relationship is more intimate than that. I want her love, not her worship. It may be that the joy of a bride and the familiar affection and trust of a wife are more pleasing to God and a better model for worship than is groveling reverence in the presence of a potentate.

Those who are born again also become God's adopted children. What does that teach us? I expect my children to treat me respectfully, but I also treasure their trust and affection. I love it when they come to me with their problems. I'm delighted when they feel so comfortable with me that they can tell me anything. I would be sad if I found that they were afraid to share some things with me. I also love to see them having a good time together, rather than saying cruel things to each other or ignoring each other—even when they aren't paying any attention to me.

My family is at its best and I am most happy when we are all enjoying each other's company. Is it possible that God is at least as interested in having us love each other and treasure each other's company in His presence as He is interested in having us worship him? When I was a boy (and later), my grandparents didn't play with me very much, but they loved to have me visit. No time of the year was better than when the whole family came to their house to share Christmas dinner.

Maybe Jesus gave us the Lord's Supper because this sort of family celebration is what most pleases God when we gather to worship. At the least, we should keep the marriage and children metaphors in mind as we consider how to worship together.

A Possible Order of Service

Here is a rather radical new order of service developed recently by my church's worship committee on the basis of my recommendations. The committee included the pastor, associate pastor, and head elder (me). It also included some of the most active musicians and two teenagers. Our goal was to develop a service during which everything is meant to bring members closer together and lift them as one up to God. Every traditional element of the service was on the table. If an element didn't fulfill our goal, we cut it or moved it to a more effective place.

During the school year our congregation is usually about 400 people, half of them teenagers at a boarding school who are in church because they are required to be. As with most churches, we begin with the various Bible study classes, then follow with the worship service. The children love their classes but find the worship service boring. Some of their parents aren't very interested in the classes, however, so they bring their children a half hour late. This is hard on both the children and the teachers.

Someone in the committee came up with the idea of having the worship service first. That way everyone is fresh, including the children. Parents learn to come on time or miss the worship service. If the service is made more interesting to children—aimed approximately at the 10-year-old—there may be no need for a children's story, as the younger children will also enjoy a service at that level. The children can all be dismissed at once at the end of the service, before the adults, and they can collect the Lamb's Offering on the way to their classes. The pastor can prepare a life-application Bible study based on his sermon, and youth and adults can study this in their classes if they choose, thus reinforcing the sermon's message.

The following schedule gives exact times merely as a guideline. I've added in parentheses what would be happening during each part of the service.

9:30 **Personal Meditation and Prayer** (people enter as they arrive, with the piano playing softly, Bible texts or hymn lyrics are projected on a screen and perhaps read aloud from the front row or read responsively)

9:45 **Congregational Singing**

9:50 **Invocation and Welcome**

9:52 **Congregational Singing**

10:15 **The Word of God** Prayer, scripture, and sermon (all by the pastor)

11:00 **Special Music** or **Hymn** (time to meditate on the sermon)

11:05 **Praises and Petitions** (the offering is announced at the time the sharing time is announced and collected during the sharing as music plays quietly; all testimonies are given from a microphone on a stand at the front of the church; people line up to share)

11:18 **Prayer of Praise and Petition** (including requested prayers)

11:20 **Lamb's Offering** (children collect the Lamb's Offering and leave from front side door to go to classes; the piano or organ plays; some parents of small children and children's teachers will leave at this time, as well)

11:25 **Announcements** (if necessary); *Mission Spotlight* (or similar activity if planned)

11:27 **Words of Blessing** (benediction)

11:28 **Postlude** or **Special Music** (no dismissal by rows)

Rationale

Here's an explanation, in random order, for the differences between the traditional order of service and the one outlined above.

1. The primary aim of the order of worship should be to bring those in the congregation into unity with God by bringing them into unity with each other through congregational singing, praying, testifying, and Scripture reading. This opens their hearts and prepares them to receive God's message to them through the words of the pastor.

2. Because congregational unity falters when people stop participating and merely watch, anything in the order of worship that disrupts participation should be removed or repositioned at the beginning or end of the service.

3. One of the aspects of worship recommended in the New Testament is personal testimony: sharing with God's people the ways one has been blessed and requesting prayer for one's needs.[1] Many churches have abandoned this. However, if we are to have unity in the church, we need to know each other's problems and know how God has been leading and blessing. If we don't know each other's needs, how can we bear each other's burdens? Hearing how God has led increases our faith.

The difficulty is knowing when to schedule this in the service. In churches already filled with love and unity, interspersing songs with personal testimony works well. In less unified churches, pausing for testimonies lowers the heat, and in any case, cool congregations get less benefit from them than do more fervent groups.

Our worship committee decided that because we needed an intense song service to build enthusiasm and open hearts, it would be better to have the testimony service at another time. We finally decided to have it after the sermon, rather than before. Our hope was that after being brought into unity with each other and lifted up to God through singing and hearing God's word through the sermon, people would be eager to share their needs and blessings publicly.

4. The distinction between preliminaries (song service and testimonies) and the "worship service" indicated by the formal entrance of the elders suggests that what comes before is not sacred or is less sacred than what follows. Yet what is sacred about the chil-

---

[1] "Everyone should feel that he has a part to act in making the Sabbath meetings interesting. You are not to come together simply as a matter of form, but for the interchange of thought, for the relation of your daily experiences, for the expression of thanksgiving, for the utterance of your sincere desire for divine enlightenment, that you may know God, and Jesus Christ, whom He has sent. Communing together in regard to Christ will strengthen the soul for life's trials and conflicts. Never think that you can be Christians and yet withdraw yourselves within yourselves. Each one is a part of the great web of humanity, and the experience of each will be largely determined by the experience of his associates.

"We do not obtain a hundredth part of the blessing we should obtain from assembling together to worship God. Our perceptive faculties need sharpening. Fellowship with one another should make us glad. With such a hope as we have, why are not our hearts all aglow with the love of God?" (Ellen G. White, *Testimonies for the Church,* vol. 6, p. 362).

dren's story, collecting the offering, or "special music"? The distinction between the less sacred and more sacred parts of the service disrupts congregational unity. This means the pastor and elders should be on the platform participating *during* the song service.

5. Congregational worship is like cooking with a pressure cooker. The heat needs to be on until the desired pressure is built up; then it needs to be adjusted. If the heat is turned off and the pressure decreases, a pressure cooker cooks no better than an ordinary kettle. Too much heat can cause an explosion, though. The worship team needs to bring the congregation up to pressure and keep it there, so a feeling of unity is reached and maintained, but doesn't explode into excess.

If the "heat" generated by congregational singing is interrupted before the pressure has built, those in the congregation may fail to become one with each other. Worship leaders often use rousing, vigorous songs of praise until the congregation is stirred up and joyful, then switch to quieter songs of adoration. This is ideal. By contrast, some worship leaders choose hymns that generate little heat, and some accompanists play without the vigor generally required for generating heat. These people can keep heart-changing worship from happening.

6. The Lamb's Offering and children's story are fun for the kids, but they decrease the pressure, so they should happen near the beginning of the song service or after the sermon. The children's story should last no more than five minutes. (It is sometimes nearly as long as the sermon.) If a worship service is lively enough and interesting enough, there may be no need for a children's story. One problem I've often noticed with children's stories is that they are over the heads of the children and aimed more at amusing teenagers and adults.

7. If we need to sing the doxology, let it be the first song we sing, or perhaps the last song before the congregational prayer and the sermon. I myself love the song, but it isn't really necessary after a half hour of songs praising God. Our worship committee decided we didn't need it.

8. The pastoral invocation and welcome should happen after the first few songs, when people have begun perking up and stragglers have wandered in. My pastor decided he would rather have one of the elders do this.

9. The collection of the offering with its concomitant organ music seriously decreases congregational fervor. One solution is to take up the offering during the song service, as a hymn is being sung. Most people can sing and pass the collection plate at the same time. Another option, if people are ushered out after the service, would be to have the ushers hold the offering plates. People would soon learn to give as they leave their rows. Ushers could also collect the offering at the door. A congregation could even increase children's love of the worship service by letting them pass the offering plates, with ushers to help them. (The more there is for children to do during worship, the more they will appreciate it.) After considering these options, our committee decided to collect the offering after the sermon, as testimonies are being given. We will have soft music playing in the background throughout this period. The music will help us maintain fervor during the pauses between testimonies.

10. "Special music" is not participatory, but a spectator sport. Therefore, if there must be "special music" (it's not required), it should occur before the song service, after the sermon instead of a closing hymn, or after the benediction as the congregation leaves. This is doubly the case if there is a need for students to perform instrumental solos (as at my church), as instrumental music is not of itself sacred, even though it may be beautiful. True beauty is a gift from God, but a beautiful instrumental solo may not be the best way to achieve congregational unity in worship, even if everyone enjoys it.

11. There is no need for an "opening hymn" accompanied by the organ, as the sermon immediately follows the song service. A closing hymn after the sermon with organ accompaniment is fine, because after the sermon is the time to release the pressure. The organ can also play a postlude.

12. Because the Scripture reading is generally only a couple

verses, let pastors read it themselves as a beginning to their sermon. (Actually, this is in line with the way it was done in Jesus' day in the synagogue.) This will make every sermon seem biblically based. Another possibility is projecting Scripture passages on a screen during the 15 minutes before the singing starts, as people are entering. This could be done while someone plays the piano quietly. Someone with a microphone in the front row could read the texts on the screen. These texts could even be used at times as a responsive reading, inviting congregational participation. Any of these will help worshipers prepare and open their hearts, rather than chat with their friends.

13. The congregational prayer should express to God the petitions and praises of the whole congregation. This means the one praying needs to be present to take notes or listen carefully as believers share what's on their hearts. Traditionally this happens just before the sermon. However, because we decided to have the testimony service after the sermon, we also decided to follow that with the congregational prayer.

14. Ideally, by the time the sermon starts, the worshipers will feel so invigorated, so close to God, and so in unity with each other that their hearts will be open to the message of the sermon and they will respond with heartfelt amens.

15. The heart of what happens before the sermon should be praise and petition (as presently happens at my church during the song service). It would be nice if people felt free to stand and read a favorite text they think would be meaningful to everyone, and there is sound biblical precedent for this. After someone expresses a serious need, one or more people could pray about it immediately. It helps if the worship leader asks people to do this. Then those asking for prayer will immediately feel like people are praying. That's not the way we are going to be doing it, but in a more fervent church, this works well.

To familiarize people with how to incorporate brief prayers and Scripture readings with the song service, it would be useful to ask several people in advance to read texts or pray, making it look spontaneous. Eventually the rest of the congregation will learn to do this without prompting.

16. Testimonies aren't effective if people can't hear them. In a small church, hearing is seldom a problem. In a larger church, deacons may need to pass around microphones, or people could be asked to come to a microphone at the front of the church. The problem with passing around microphones is that it can slow down the service and so decrease congregational fervor. The problem with having a microphone at the front is that it takes more courage to walk up and use it. I think, though, that people would get used to lining up to testify, and they would soon realize that publicly thanking God for His blessings can be an inspiration to everyone. Unity grows when we all know each other's trials and victories. If we are all parts of one body, the hand needs to know when the foot is sore.

Testifying has two purposes. First, people testify to praise God for what He has done. When they do this, everyone is edified. Everyone can praise God together. But if people can't hear, they won't be edified. Second, people solicit prayers because of some difficulty they are going through. They do this because they crave the prayers and support of their brothers and sisters. But if people can't hear the request, they can't pray about the problem.

17. God's temple on earth is not the church building, but the church—the believers themselves, both individually and corporately. Paul was right when he told the listeners on Mars Hill, "The God who made the world and everything in it is the Lord of heaven and earth and does not live in temples built by hands" (Acts 17:24, NIV). The only holiness in the "sanctuary" itself is a result of God's holy people having gathered together there. True, they have come to be with God and bask in His presence—the presence they can feel when they become one—so this isn't the time to neglect Him and chat about worldly things. They should focus on unity and fellowship, both with God and with each other. However, silent rev-

erence is not necessarily the best way to accomplish this.[2] The injunction to "walk softly in the sanctuary" is appropriate only in that when God's people are gathered together, they *are* the sanctuary. They shouldn't be distracted from achieving corporate unity.

18. Unity is built when God's people develop a relationship with each other, when they truly care for each other and carry each other's burdens, and this is Christ's desire for them. Thus, it is entirely appropriate for God's people to stand or sit in the "sanctuary" after the worship service and converse. There is no biblical reason for this to be postponed until people are in the foyer. To encourage this building of relationship through conversation, it might be useful to stop dismissing people by rows. After the benediction, the pastor might actually announce that "now it's time to worship through fellowship." Traditionally pastors greet people at the church door as they leave. Our new service, however, has everyone leaving at once, so instead of causing a bottleneck at the door, our pastor plans to stay near the platform so those who want to speak with him can have easier access.

19. The congregational singing will be most conducive of unity and openheartedness if not accompanied by the organ. Piano works best for hymns, while both piano and guitars work well for praise songs. A cappella singing is especially nice with slow hymns, as it encourages harmonizing. Some songs are best sung slowly and prayerfully. Most songs are best sung vigorously and joyously. There's no place for bland, unfeeling, or joyless singing in congregational worship. Members should be encouraged to enter into the joy of their Lord and sing with spirit and in the Spirit. It's better to sing a cappella entirely than to use musicians who can't play vigorously.

20. Congregational singing will work best if there is an active song leader, rather than someone who merely stands in front and

---

[2] "The evil of formal worship cannot be too strongly depicted, but no words can properly set forth the deep blessedness of genuine worship. When human beings sing with the spirit and the understanding, heavenly musicians take up the strain and join in the song of thanksgiving" (Ellen G. White, *Testimonies for the Church*, vol. 9, pp. 143, 144).

chooses songs. Everyone should be able to hear the leader while singing. Song leaders don't need to be talented singers. Effective ones, though, do need to be leaders. At the church camp meeting I attend every summer, there's a retired pastor who often leads the singing. His voice isn't great, but everyone loves his boundless enthusiasm and infectious joy. He is by far our favorite song leader, and when he leads, we sing our hearts out. It's a wonderful experience.

How Do We Change Without Alienating Members?

What follows is going to be aimed at pastors, but every reader will find it useful. So, pastor, perhaps you've read the whole book to this point, you agree with most of what I've written, and you are eager to change the order of service right away, build congregational unity, and enjoy true worship. It's not that easy.

Forcing a new way of worship on people who glare at visitors who accidentally sit in "their pew" is a great way to divide a church or lose a job or reputation. If you aren't careful, when you try to change things some members will leave or stop supporting the church. If you try something dramatic but fail, people will be less ready to try again. If you don't have the courage to go all the way, you may not notice much difference in your congregation, and many will assume changes in worship don't work. If you back away from proposed changes, you may lose those who like me are desperately unhappy with a lukewarm worship that seems to them blasphemous.

On the other hand, if there is little feeling of unity and love during worship at your church, you may have already lost many members. If the situation can be reversed, some of these may return. Visitors will be much more likely to want to join. Evangelism will be more successful. Children and youth will begin participating in worship. Enthusiastic members will support the church's mission in every way. What's more, the goal is to achieve what God asks us to achieve, not merely to do something new and exciting.

So how do you make these changes? I hate committee meetings, but the truth is that committees sometimes come up with good ideas and good solutions. You need to set up a worship committee to consider changes. Choose for it people with hearts for God and people with ideas. Ideally, several generations should be represented, including youth and retired people, but avoid those who are set in their ways. You need people who are willing to put God and the needs of the church first, no matter what their personal tastes may be. It also helps if at least some of the members are musicians sympathetic to the type of worship you envision. People with influence over church members are also useful.

A good first step is to ask the committee to study what the Bible teaches about music and worship. What are the principles? What are the examples? Are the examples applicable to us? This book can help answer questions like these. (Pay special attention to the passages at the beginning of chapters.) This may require several meetings. People like me will be getting impatient, but it's important to keep everyone on board, rather than losing them.

Next, ask the committee to study your current order of service and discuss each element. Is it necessary? Is it biblically required? Is it effective, or is there a better way to do it? Does it draw the congregation closer to each other and closer to God? This may also take several weeks.

Then it's time for the committee to begin thinking up solutions, ways of doing things that will lead to the desired goal of unity. You may be amazed by some of the creative ideas.

At some point, church members are going to hear about this committee, and some will be worried. Some of those who are worried may not have the courage or honesty to come to you directly. Some will feed the gossip mill. Among those who will be worried are those who are quite happy with the service the way it is, those who believe the order of service was set in place by God at Sinai, and those who see the committee members as dangerous radicals intent on setting up a "celebration church," a "charismatic church," a "megachurch," or some similar supposed abomination.

You may also face suspicion from those with a lot of musical training. These people should be your allies in your quest for life-changing worship, but sometimes they have a substantial investment in high-quality instrumental and vocal performance and fear that the proposed service will no longer move them or need their help.

These people will need to be visited and reassured. Ask for their ideas—they may have some good ones. Present to them the Bible teaching on worship and music. Help them catch your vision of what true worship could be at your church. Remind them of the overwhelming importance of retaining our youth, bringing them to salvation, and turning them into disciples and leaders. Urge them to set aside their own preferences for the good of the church. Ask them to give the church time to try something new. Promise them that after it's been given a fair trial, there will be time for evaluation.

(I want to remind you again that if you lack the courage to go all the way lest someone be offended, if you decide simply to tweak the present order of service a bit and see what that does, you will probably be disappointed. Moving things around a little won't change lives. The need is for a radical transformation from lukewarm worship—false worship—to true, wholehearted, openhearted, life-filling, life-changing worship, whatever it takes to get there. Once they've experienced it, whatever the form, few members will want to go back. But first they have to experience it.)

It will also be necessary to preach about true worship. Prepare people for the changes. Make true worship seem so attractive that members begin longing for it. Help them see the difference between human traditions and what the Bible actually requires or suggests. It may also be a good idea at some point to have a church business meeting for questions and answers. There may be significant questions the committee hasn't yet considered. Also, many people may need only a couple answers before they are ready to give the new worship service a try. I don't recommend asking the church to vote on this. Ideally, the church board has voted on the worship committee's report and is solidly behind the pastor. Asking for a church vote, however, is a good way to polarize the congregation.

You may have noticed that I haven't said much in this chapter about the type of music to be used in this new worship service. That will depend on your congregation. In this book I've done my best to show that many forms of music with Christian lyrics can glorify God. In a congregation with few or no youth but a problem with lukewarm music, a good song leader and pianist could lead a revival out of the church hymnal. A fun alternative would be bringing in some of the youth favorites from 50 years ago. As the older folks start singing more vigorously for a longer period, the change in the congregation will become evident, and young people will begin joining in.

Some congregations may take special delight in Southern gospel favorites, such as "Precious Lord, Take My Hand," "There's a New Name Written Up in Glory," or "Just a Closer Walk With Thee." In these congregations banjos, mandolins, and fiddles may be welcomed as accompaniment. African-American congregations have a number of related gospel favorites and a reputation for singing them well. Here brass and woodwind players may accompany the songs. Spanish-speaking congregations also have rich musical traditions on which they can draw. All of these styles and all of these instruments are blessed by God when they are used to sing his praises.

In my own congregation, where we have 200 young people, it will probably be easier to encourage enthusiastic participation with lively praise songs.[3] These can be played by some of the pi-

---

[3] Some of the praise songs my children enjoy singing enthusiastically include Darlene Zschech's "Shout to the Lord," Jack Hayford's "Majesty," Scott Underwood's "Take My Life" (sometimes called "Holiness"), Martin Smith's "I Could Sing of Your Love Forever," Paul Baloche's "Open the Eyes of My Heart," Graham Kendrick's "Shine, Jesus, Shine," Naida Hearn's "Jesus, Name Above All Names," Lenny LeBlanc and Paul Baloche's "Above All," Michael W. Smith and Deborah D. Smith's "Great Is the Lord," and Michael O'Shields' "I Will Call Upon the Lord." Some of these should be sung two or three times in a row. Some are quiet. Others are best appreciated in the light of Psalm 47:1. All are songs of true biblical praise, many with lyrics closely based on Scripture.

anists or by a combination of guitars and electronic keyboard.[4]

Whatever the music, it should be carefully rehearsed, not so much because it needs to sound professional as because it needs to flow in an attractive way from song to song, without long pauses. Pianists are used to playing introductions to songs as song leaders give the page numbers, but young people with guitars have less experience with this. Musicians, including the song leader, of course, should generally figure out in advance who will play the introduction and what it will sound like and how many times they are going to play a song. I'm sure God accepts praise played by kids who are just learning an instrument, but they should be encouraged to practice and improve. (The same goes, of course, for the pianist in the rural church who after 20 years can still play only six songs and can't keep time: practice.)

In many churches there are very few musicians, but in larger churches there may be several dozen. In these churches it may be a good idea to set up several music teams. Each team would practice on its own, learning songs and deciding how they will be played. They would have assigned weeks to prepare for, perhaps once a month or every two months. Different teams might focus on excellence in different styles of music. For example, in my church our 200 students go home to their families one weekend in five. This would be a good time to have a music team that leads us in favorite hymns.

It would also be nice if, say, one talented guitarist in the church were assigned to help kids learn to play. These young people could

---

[4] Many acoustic guitars these days have electric pickups built into them. If a church is going to use guitars and keyboard very often, it might be a good idea to provide a panel on the platform that will accommodate both microphone jacks and guitar jacks, connected directly to the public-address system mixing board. This way there would be no need for separate guitar and keyboard amplifiers or microphones for guitars, and the volume and mixing could be controlled from the back of the church. The guitar that seems too loud during the preservice sound check in an empty room may sound just right when people are singing quietly and too quiet when people are singing loudly, but it's difficult for people playing on the platform to know how they sound in the back of the room.

themselves become a music team that plays occasionally for the congregation but also leads singing in their respective Bible classes.

We Can Do It

Far too many people attend church because they think it is the right thing to do. Far too many young people attend church because they are required to. It doesn't have to be that way. When the 6-year-olds in the congregation feel the need to stretch out on the pew beside their parents and the teenagers open their church magazines, we've lost their attention and bored them. They are no longer worshiping. If we watch where this happens in the service, we may discover what needs to be changed. Worship isn't only for adults. If the worship service doesn't interest young people, why would they want to return when they are older? Do we dare exclude our children in order to cling to our traditional ways of worship?

I dream of a church service people attend because it's the best part of their week. I dream of people coming to worship because they feel that the church members are their brothers and sisters, people they know and care about. I dream of visitors feeling surrounded by love and filled with love for others and for God. I dream of their wanting to come back every week.

I dream of children begging their parents to take them to church because it's so much fun. I dream of a church service where people sing their lungs out because they are so full of joy and gratitude, no matter what sort of song they are singing. I dream of singing and praising that lifts people higher and higher, closer and closer to God, until they feel they can look into His eyes. I dream of people so overcome by the power of God as they sing that they dissolve in tears of joy or repentance.

I dream of people being so filled with the Spirit and so open-hearted as a result of their participation that they hear the sermon as if it were God's direct word to them. I dream of people making commitments to God as they listen, submitting to God's working in their lives.

I dream of people so invigorated by communal worship that they devote their lives to serving others and proclaiming the good news of salvation.

It can happen.

Chapter 9

The Church I Long to See

As you know, it was because of an illness that I first preached
the gospel to you. Even though my illness was a
trial to you, you did not treat me with contempt or scorn.
Instead, you welcomed me as if I were an angel of God,
as if I were Christ Jesus himself!
—Galatians 4:13, 14, NIV

If you bite and devour one another,
beware lest you be consumed by one another!
—Galatians 5:15, NKJV

Brethren, if a man is overtaken in any trespass, you who are
spiritual restore such a one in a spirit of gentleness, considering
yourself lest you also be tempted. Bear one another's burdens, and
so fulfill the law of Christ. For if anyone thinks himself to be
something, when he is nothing, he deceives himself. But let each
one examine his own work, and then he will have rejoicing in
himself alone, and not in another.
—Galatians 6:1-4

The Lord's servant must not be quarrelsome but kindly to everyone,
an apt teacher, patient, correcting opponents with gentleness. God
may perhaps grant that they will repent and come to know the
truth, and that they may escape from the snare of the devil, having
been held captive by him to do his will.
—2 Timothy 2:24-26, NRSV

Music has divided for far too long. This book
has been an attempt to show that such division is unnecessary, harmful, and in opposition to Jesus' prayer that His followers would live

together in unity. What follows is not specifically about music, but about the unity of the body of Christ, the people of God. It lays out my dreams of what the church could be if we were willing, what God longs for it to be. Compared to unity, the music wars are of little importance.

When an early version of this chapter was published as an article, the editors changed words such as "crippled" and "handicapped" to what they considered less pejorative terms, much to my dismay. I hope those who are physically disabled will understand that I'm writing here about spiritual disabilities and not take offense at my words. Those who are physically disabled are well aware of their disabilities, and calling them cripples won't help them deal with their difficulties. Most of us who are spiritually and psychologically disabled, however, don't realize it, so in order to make it very clear, I'm using terms I've learned not to use when working with the physically disabled. Please forgive me.

Spiritually Handicapped

A few years ago my back failed me. I couldn't stand or sit or lie on my side for more than a few seconds without great pain. The only comfortable position was flat on my back, floating on narcotics.

The doctor in the pain clinic injected cortisone into my spine. The chiropractor tweaked my vertebrae. The elders anointed me. There was no apparent effect.

I feared I would never stand or even sit again. When my wife took me to the doctor's office, she carried a foam pallet for me. I lay on the waiting room floor like the man at the Pool of Bethesda, waiting for an angel to stir the waters.

Finally, after six weeks, I went to a neurosurgeon. He said, "Stand on your left leg and rise up onto your toes."

My brain said, "I will," but my body didn't respond. *O wretched man that I am! Who will deliver me from this body of death?*

The surgeon said, "If you're willing, I'll operate tomorrow."

"I'm willing," I said. "The surgery scares me, but it can't be worse than the way I am now."

When I awoke, the sciatic nerve pain was gone. The next morning I sat up to eat breakfast, then slowly walked the hospital halls, praising God.

But I didn't run and jump. That took time. First came several months of exercising numb muscles, waiting for nerves to recover. I still get cramps in my left calf that remind me where I've been.

In our spiritual life, it's not enough to submit to the knife of the Great Surgeon. We also need the guiding hand of the Great Physical Therapist. He gives us exercises that strengthen us. He asks us to come (Matt. 11:28). He tells us to go (Matt. 28:18-20). He gives us challenges (1 Cor. 10:13). He asks us to follow (Matt. 4:19). The exercises are progressive, building us without discouraging us (Phil. 4:13).

We are told, "Therefore, strengthen your feeble arms and weak knees. 'Make level paths for your feet,' so that the lame may not be disabled, but rather healed" (Heb. 12:12, 13, NIV; see also verses 1-11).

My late grandmother had an arthritic knee replaced. She was soon walking a mile a day—more than she'd been able to walk for years.

But she didn't continue with her bending and stretching exercises because they hurt. Scar tissue formed around her new joint. Soon she could no longer walk more than a few yards, and the pain returned.

Spiritually, a lot of us are in a similar condition.

I've been born again. I've surrendered myself completely to God. What I most love to talk about and think about and read about is Jesus. I want to be like Jesus, but in many ways I'm not.

People read my articles and listen to my tapes and attend my classes, and this makes them want to be like Jesus. They assume that I must be like Jesus, because I talk about Him. But in many ways I'm not.

I've been very shy ever since I was a little boy. I don't want to be shy, but I am. I'm not shy in front of a crowd or with people I know, but it's very difficult for me to meet people or visit people.

Recently an old man in my church died. He had been sick for a year. In all that time I didn't visit him. I *should have* visited him. *Jesus* would have visited him, and I *want* to be like Jesus. Being shy is not a good enough excuse.

When I was a schoolboy, some of my classmates teased me a lot, and this made me very unhappy. I was sure I was worthless, and even today it's hard for me to believe that people would want to meet me or really want me to visit them in the hospital or come over for dinner.

Being teased and feeling worthless and not feeling as if anyone was standing up for me or willing to help me made me angry, but I was too shy to respond angrily to the ones who teased me. Instead, I yelled at my parents.

Even after I got married, when I was under a lot of pressure I got angry and yelled at my family, even though I considered my marriage a very happy one, and even though it wasn't my family that caused my stress. I never yelled at the people who caused the pressure. Yelling at home was simply letting off the day's steam.

When I was born again, though, I gave my anger at the world to God, and He took it away. But sometimes when I'm tense I still yell, even though my anger lasts only a few seconds, and even though I immediately apologize. I don't want to yell. I love my family so much, and I want to always be like Jesus when I talk to them. But sometimes I still get angry.

Why does this happen? If I've given my heart to God, why do I still struggle with what I used to be?

Here's the answer. Part of what I am is in my genes. I inherited these genes from my parents, and I can't change them. My genes affect the way I perceive reality and the way I act. My parents never yelled, but I inherited shyness and my introverted nature.

Part of what I am is because of what has happened to me in the past. It can be very hard to escape from one's past. God can heal us so the past doesn't hurt, but the effects of our past may still be there and affect our actions sometimes.

Also, it is very hard to see ourselves as others see us. I tend to see myself as wise and kind and very competent, a person with an answer to every problem. However, other people sometimes see me as proud and selfish and intimidating. I don't see myself that way, and that's certainly not how I want others to see me, but it can be very difficult to actually be what we believe ourselves to be.

Psychologically and spiritually speaking, I want to stand tall for God. I want to walk straight. Instead, it seems, I don't *walk* with God. I *limp* with God. I want to support others. But I need others to support me, too. Admitting this is like admitting that when it comes to being a Christian, I'm an utter failure. It fills me with shame.

God's church is *filled* with people who limp. God calls us to support each other, so the church can be strong and spread the good news of salvation.

Can the Body of Christ Be Handicapped?

There was a time when we pegged some people as "crippled" and avoided them. Today we're learning to see the disabled as "differently abled."

We've found that in many cases, providing a motorized wheelchair, a car with hydraulic controls, sidewalk ramps, and barrier-free restrooms frees someone we've seen as a "cripple" to become a corporate president, or at least have some personal freedom and control.

In society we've learned to work around problems and make use of what abilities a person may have. We're learning to treat the physically and mentally challenged as human beings who can succeed and contribute, given a little extra help.

Physically, I'm not crippled. Spiritually and psychologically, though, I am crippled—like you. We are all crippled. We are all handicapped. We are all disabled. We are all challenged. We are all suffering from spiritual birth defects, and we all have spiritual and psychological scars from childhood accidents.

The apostle Paul writes, in essence, "The things my heart says 'Do!' my flesh doesn't do, and when my heart says 'Don't do it!' my flesh does it anyway" (Rom. 7:14-25). That's not an excuse for sin or a license to sin boldly, but the human condition, the way we are. It's an inspired commentary on the way things are with us, and in our hearts we know it's true.

We have not yet learned, though, that every part of the body of Christ but the Head is also handicapped. It's time we realized that instead of shooting our spiritual cripples, or jeering at them, we need to fit them with braces and crutches and put them to work doing whatever their handicaps allow.

In the world we are discovering that if we get to know them and learn how to enable them, we may find that the differently abled are wonderful, delightful, capable people.

In the church we often shun our spiritually and psychologically disabled rather than help them. There are some disabilities we accept, true, but there are others we do not. With some disabilities it's "Trip once and you're out." Imagine if we did that with the physically disabled.

We especially do not want pastors who are handicapped. When we see a person with a withered hand, we don't assume the rest of that person is withered. But when a pastor with a limp trips and falls, why does the congregation assume the pastor is crippled to the core?

Here's my main point: Instead of rejecting a whole person because of a spiritual weakness in one part of the body or mind, we need to help the person deal with that problem for the sake of the health of the body of Christ.

We may even need to make allowances for that problem, to work around it. We may need to understand that some people will always have their problem.

Some people make a nearly full recovery, but will always walk with a limp. Completely removing a colon cancer may leave one with a colostomy bag. Even when a person returns to health following major surgery by the Great Physician, there may be an unsightly scar, and that scar may ache a little when the weather changes.

The church is a rehabilitation hospital where people come to get back on their feet, and a good rehabilitation hospital has to be barrier-free, or patients get hurt. A lot of patients with strokes make remarkable improvement in rehabilitation hospitals, but they don't necessarily make a full recovery.

Jeering at Cripples

It's useful to distinguish between being handicapped by lack of talent and being handicapped by a tendency toward some type of sin. Let's look first at those crippled by mediocrity.

In the Christian college I attended I had a classmate who had remarkable self-confidence, but because of an accident at birth he lurched when he walked, had bizarre facial tics, and slurred his speech. We mimicked him. We laughed when he asked out pretty girls—who of course turned him down. We smirked when he wanted to be a physician, and again when he later tried to sell life insurance. We rolled our eyes when he responded to an altar call, bawled out his personal testimony, and was baptized. We thought he should be working at Goodwill Industries or ringing a bell for the Salvation Army, not going to college. Shame on us!

I've come to realize that when church members criticize or gossip, they are nearly always jeering at cripples, laughing at people for being disabled. Why? Because these church members are complaining about people who may be doing the best they can, instead of making their paths straight so they don't trip and fall.

The most boring pastors may spend 30 hours polishing a sermon. Perhaps they don't visit members because like me they're shy, and intruding into peoples' lives terrifies them.

That woman with the appalling dress may have saved for months to buy the cut-rate fabric she sewed herself.

That man with three hundred hairs carefully combed over his shining dome may be fooling no one but himself, but do we realize his intense embarrassment at being follicly challenged? How can we help him feel like part of the family, someone who will be accepted even if he's completely bald?

That self-celebrated soprano may be singing flat, but have we heard ourselves lately?

Again, I am not talking here about tendencies to sin or weaknesses that interfere with our walk with God. These are mere matters of taste and talent in the body of Christ. Are we so upstanding that we're entitled to verbally kick these cripples' crutches?

Yet pastors have lost their livelihoods because of their haircuts or suits or accents, because of a chance word on a bad day or a tentative position tested in a worship talk. What happened to "the benefit of the doubt"? What happened to forgiveness? What happened to making allowances for people who are doing the best they can?

We have ostracized people both for buying a Mercedes and for driving a rusty clunker, for wearing jeans to church and for wearing a suit. We have avoided fellow Christians because they are too smart or too dumb, too pretty or too ugly, too rich or too poor, too neat or too sloppy.

We must be willing to call sin by its right name, and we must be willing to train the trainable. We must also, however, make endless allowances for the leopards among us who cannot change their spots, for annoying but unconscious mannerisms, for those whose offensively blunt habit of speech has been passed down for generations.

Yes, these people walk with a limp. But does it matter? Looked in the mirror lately?

What's *Your* Handicap?

My friend Jason rides a motorized wheelchair, but he's a deep thinker and knows his Bible. His legs don't work, but his spirit walks with God.

Last time I saw him he asked me to pray that his problems won't make him grow impatient and snap at those caring for him. That momentary lack of gratitude and an occasional slide into depression are the spiritual handicaps he bears because of his physical challenges.

What handicap interferes with your own walk with God? Where are you tempted to sin?

Perhaps like me you are generally kind and peaceful, but sometimes you grow impatient, anger boils up, and you say something you shouldn't.

Perhaps you are so shy you can hardly bear to talk out loud, so you refuse to tell the good news to those who ask.

Perhaps you walk with God nearly all the time, but you have a limp called lust, and you are easily led away by pornography.

Perhaps you love money and don't want to share with those in need.

Perhaps your handicap is your fear of inviting someone home for dinner.

Perhaps you are handicapped by prejudice against ethnic groups other than your own.

Perhaps you are crippled by a spirit of criticism or doubt that makes it hard for you to believe the Bible is God's word to you.

Perhaps you are crippled by biblical literalism or an inability to accept any Bible version but the King James.

Perhaps you are disabled by a tendency to argue during Bible study for the sake of argument.

Perhaps you have been crippled by certain theological ideas you learned somewhere.

Perhaps you are disabled by a dislike of praise songs in preference to the grand old hymns—or vice versa.

Perhaps you are handicapped by your appetite, as seen by your high-piled plate at church potluck dinners.

Perhaps you are disabled by mental sloth, by your refusal to devote yourself to Bible study and prayer.

Perhaps you are a perfectionist and are handicapped by self-deception or egotism, thinking you can walk alone, claiming you can walk without falling, without sinning, and scorning those who can't.

Perhaps you are addicted to television.

Perhaps you are addicted to sports.

Perhaps you are addicted to hobbies.

Perhaps you are addicted to housecleaning or yardwork.

Yes, these are disabilities. If they are not treated, they all lead to sin. But consider this: some disabilities you can overcome, such as stuttering or lisping. Some disabilities you can learn to work around, such as a paralyzed muscle. If you learn to surmount your spiritual disabilities, you may become a role model for others. Those who walk with a limp may walk more slowly, but they walk.

What's more, those who have overcome their handicaps make the best teachers. They can tell us what worked for them, what to expect, when to expect it.

Even those who haven't completely recovered make good teachers. Stroke victims who have learned tricks for feeding themselves or reaching items on high shelves have knowledge worth sharing.

Born Again—But Still a Cripple?

We agree that in our glorified bodies in the new earth there will no more suffering, no more tears, no more disabilities, no more sin. But what about being born again? If we are truly born again, born of God, can we still be disabled?

Sometimes God heals our infirmities. Sometimes God gives us strength to overcome them. Sometimes he helps us bear them without sin. Rebirth is life-changing and liberating, but primarily spiritual. Any physical changes are usually the effect of receiving a renewed spirit within us.

A friend of mine argues that because homosexuality is sinful, it is not possible to be both born again and tempted by homosexuality. The handicap model suggests otherwise. Those who are reborn are sometimes freed, but others may be tempted by what they long to escape. They may even fall and need to be helped up.

I've read that many priests who sexually abuse boys were themselves abused the same way. That abuse crippled them. Most people who beat their children were themselves beaten when they were children. Those beatings crippled them. That doesn't mean they can't say no when they are tempted, but it's much harder for them to say no than it is for most people in the church. Let's take a really extreme case. If child abusers fall, are we willing to forgive them if they repent and help them back onto their feet?*

It's very easy for me to avoid drinking alcohol, but for an alcoholic who hasn't had a drink in a decade, the temptation may still be very powerful. If alcoholics returns briefly to drink, can the church forgive them if they are sorry?

There are many temptations easily avoided by most church members, yet nearly impossible for other members to withstand. Those areas of weakness are their handicaps. They need special help in dealing with these temptations. They are walking with God, but walking with a limp. They need us to pick them up when they trip and fall.

My friend Jason is born again, but still in a wheelchair and still sometimes impatient. God has healed his spirit, but not his body, and even his spirit still needs exercising so it can grow strong. Should it be surprising, then, if God heals a homosexual's spirit, yet does not necessarily remove the handicap drawing the person to others of the same sex?

To give in to the urge would be a sin. God offers strength to resist the temptation, and with God's strength the temptation can indeed be resisted, the handicap transcended. But what if the person lets go of God's hand for a moment and stumbles? Should we kick the cripple or help the person stand again?

If a woman walking with crutches falls down, we don't expel her from the church. If a child with epilepsy has a seizure, she is not shunned, but helped. How quick should the body of Christ be to amputate its weaker members? Is it better to have a shriveled leg in a brace or to cut it off and have no leg?

Remember my aching back? Our surrender to the Great Physician is like signing surgical consent forms. It frees Him to do

---

* I realize that for many readers forgiving a child molester seems utterly impossible, and even wrong. I admit that I am deliberately trying to shock, choosing a very difficult example. I'm not advocating that child abusers be casually forgiven and allowed to continue unpunished. But if they repent, doesn't the Bible teach that God will forgive? And if God will forgive, aren't we also obligated to forgive?

surgery on us, to cut and sew. When we wake up we are new creations, in a way, as if reborn. The old pain may be gone, but we're still weak. Our muscles have atrophied. We have to learn to walk again. And we still have cramps now and then. Paul tells us he did (Rom. 7:14-25; 2 Cor. 12:7-10).

Being born again changes us from being sick with a deadly disease to being convalescent. It begins the restoration of God's image in us. But convalescents often have setbacks.

It's not our place to create a master race by purging the weak and fallen in our church, leaving only the strong. God strengthens people one step at a time. We should do the same.

This is not the same as condoning sin or welcoming sin. It is Jesus who tells us to pray, "Forgive us our debts as we forgive our debtors." It is Jesus who cautions us, "Let him who is without sin cast the first stone." And we are all cripples.

Sinners Anonymous

Alcoholics Anonymous does not condone alcoholism, but its primary purpose is to minister to alcoholics and their families. Alcoholics come to the meetings, admit what they are, ask their "higher power" for help, and are strengthened by the support of other alcoholics who, likewise, are determined to be free of the slavery of alcohol.

Why can't our church be a sort of Sinners Anonymous? Why can't it be a place where a woman can stand up and say, "I saw a really handsome man in a restaurant last Tuesday, and after he flirted with me I spent the afternoon daydreaming about him. God forgive me"? A place where those nearby lay their hands on her shoulders while someone prays for her?

What if someone stands up and says, "I don't know what got into me. I haven't had a drink in 10 years, but I went into a bar and bought a beer. Please pray for me"? Could we pray and forgive and comfort, or would we first have to take it to the church board and remove the person from church office for a year, just in case?

What if a boy says, "Please pray for me—I lost my temper and yelled at my mom"? And what if he confesses that sin every week for a year (James 5:16; Matt. 18:22)? Can we still forgive? More than that, can we patiently mentor and disciple him, encourage and praise him?

Are we that willing to support and strengthen those addicted to sin who want to break the habit? Well, what about the marriage counselor who has, by the grace of God, said no to extramarital sexual temptations for 15 years, but turns briefly from God and falls? He is badly battered and in despair. Do we throw our arms around him and help him start over or shiver with disgust?

If a teenage member of the body of Christ gets pregnant but is heartily sorry and in need of our help, must we treat her the same as the teenager who moves in with her boyfriend and argues that it's not wrong (1 Cor. 1:1-5 versus 2 Cor. 2:5-8; John 8:11)?

When pastors fall, what responsibility do their congregations bear? Do they provide a group to support them? Could they share their struggles, much less confess their sins, to their congregation, without jeopardizing their livelihood? Did the members see them as recovering sinners always one false step from a relapse, or somehow imagine they were completely cured from sin?

God Hires the Handicapped

It's not a sin to have a mental or physical disability, even though in some cases disabilities may be a result of sin, or at least of living in a fallen world.

The spiritual and psychological handicaps I'm talking about are also not sins, but disabilities we bear because we live in a fallen world, a world of birth defects. The sin is not in the tendency or the temptation, but in the giving in (1 Cor. 10:13). Even Jesus was continually tested, just as we are, yet those temptations were not in themselves sin (Heb. 4:15).

We are a church of cripples, and we are constantly falling down, but we are also the body of Christ.

When Jesus dwelt among us, "he took up our infirmities and

carried our sorrows" (Isa. 53:4, NIV). He was the Son of God and the Son of Man at the same time. Today our heavenly Head is still attached to an infirm and sorrowing body—us.

We are crippled, yet we are His body. So He will say, "If you're willing, I'll operate right now." If our weak legs fail us and we fall, He will prop us up. He will exercise us and strengthen us. He will enable us. He will not give up on us unless we insist on amputating ourselves from His body, though even then He is willing to sew us back on.

If our Head takes this attitude toward us, what attitude should we take toward each other?

Imagine the First Church of the Spiritually Handicapped eagerly limping along in the footsteps of its Head. The spiritual and psychological quadriplegics are giving directions while the spiritual Down's children push their wheelchairs. The deaf are leading the blind. People are always tripping and falling, but others are always helping them up and urging them on. The dwarfs are lifted up so they can see. The giants are supported so they don't stumble. The closer everyone presses together, the less often they fall. The farther they walk together, following the Head, the stronger they grow.

Alone, we *all* walk with a limp.

I'm tired of limping. Let's support each other as Jesus asked us to do. Let's lift each other from the ground when we fall. Let's lift each other up to Jesus.

Last year I sent these ideas to an old girlfriend of mine. She hasn't been to church in nearly 30 years. She wrote back, "If there really were a church like that, I would join it."

The world is full of people who would join a church like that. If we are willing to support each other and follow our Head, Jesus, we can *be* that church.

When we *are* that church, we will bring glory to God.

When we *are* that church, every lonely person will want to join with us.

When we *are* that church, every person searching for God will find that He is with us.

When we *are* that church, there will not only be room for others, but there will be room for *us*.

After all, we are also weak. We also need people to lift us up.

The First Church of the Spiritually Handicapped is not only for *others,* but for *us*.

Appendix 1

Be What You See

A *disciple* is not above the teacher, nor a slave
above the master; it is enough for the *disciple* to be
like the teacher, and the slave like the master.
—Matthew 10:24, 25

Beloved, we are God's children now; what we will be
has not yet been revealed. What we do know is this:
when he is revealed, we will be *like him,*
for we will see him as he is.
—1 John 3:2

There's something about a real star that makes you want to be what you see.

When she heard Niña's first big hit on the radio, Olivia knew there was something special about Niña, something that called out to her. When she saw Niña's photo on her CD, Olivia felt that here was a person she'd like to be.

Niña started showing up in the fanzines, and Olivia began clipping her photos and taping them to her bathroom mirror. As she stood in front of the mirror, her eyes would turn from Niña to herself, looking for similarities. *Perhaps the cheekbones? Don't our lips have almost the same shape? When I suck in my cheeks a little they look like Niña's,* I think.

It wasn't that Niña was so beautiful—she really looked pretty ordinary, when it came down to it. But there was something so bold, so brash, so confident in the way she carried herself, as if she were her own person and didn't care about other people or what they thought. That look seemed to capture what Olivia felt inside. She wanted it to show on the outside, too. She wanted to be like Niña.

Olivia had her hair cut like Niña's: shaved on the left side, shagged on top, and shoulder length and wet-looking on the right and in the back. It looked great. Her friends said they loved it. In the mirror she practiced that Niña sneer, and she tried to hold it on her face all day.

She studied Niña's clothes, but searched in vain for ones like them. Then she found a fashion magazine with a big spread on Niña. It even said where she bought each item and how much it cost.

Olivia took a lot of money out of her savings account, took a bus to New York, and came back with no money and a wardrobe just like Niña's.

Another magazine had a step-by-step guide to how Niña did her makeup. This was priceless! Olivia bought all the right brand names and colors and practiced for days till she had it down. *Really,* she thought, *I could pass for Niña's little sister.* Her friends agreed, even the guys.

As Niña's career progressed—more CDs, more hits, a movie— her style developed, and Olivia's kept pace. When Niña bleached her hair, leaving a quarter inch of black roots, Olivia did, too. Her mom cried, but her friends stuck by her.

When Niña had a silver stud put in her nose, Olivia did too. It made her boyfriend uncomfortable. He told her it looked like she had a big zit on her nose. She didn't talk to him for several days.

Niña had an eyebrow pierced. The photo showed a neat little ring with a tiny sapphire in it. Olivia got one, too. Her boyfriend said it looked like she'd cut her eyebrow in a fight and had to have stitches. He was right, but she wasn't about to admit it. They broke up.

When Niña had her tongue pierced and a barbell put in, Olivia was surprised. How could Niña sing with that thing in her mouth? The closeup photo looked pretty sick. It definitely seemed to be more about pain than beauty.

It turned out, though, that having her own barbell put through her tongue hurt Olivia less than she expected. Some of the more radical kids at school started inviting Olivia to hang out with them. This rather startled her, because she didn't see herself (or Niña) as their sort. Her own old friends seemed somehow more distant, less friendly. Her dad said the barbell in her tongue made him sick to his stomach.

"Be what you see"? When it came to looking like Niña, Olivia had gone about as far as she could. When she looked in the mirror now, it was Niña who seemed to sneer back at her. When she walked down the hall at school, she kept hearing the name "Niña" in conversations behind her back, or at least she seemed to.

She had set up an image to her idol. She had worshipped the image. She had become the image. Her mind was filled with it.

But Niña's next big move, at the height of her glory, was a step too far for Olivia. Where Niña went then, Olivia was not willing to follow. The scarlet ribbons in Niña's hair, the dripping rose petals on the bathroom tiles, were splashed across the front page. It was the long goodbye. She was sleeping the big sleep. By her own choice, by her own hand, Niña had ceased to be.

When a pop icon is smashed, there are predictable results. There are a few copycat suicides. There are lots of flowers at the funeral. There are big articles in *Time* and *Newsweek*. There are dedicated Web sites where the computer literate post gory photos and rancid poetry.

There were no tabloid cover stories when Jesus died, no fields of wreathed flowers, no mournful voice-overs on the TV news coverage of the funeral. But Jesus was a real star, the biggest star of all.

In Revelation 13 we find out about the image of the satanic beast. The rule is this: Worship it or die. We ourselves can be images of the beast. We can look and talk and act and think so much like Satan that when people look at us, they think they're seeing him.

Lots of people do that. They want to be "bad," "edgy," dangerous, threatening. They live "cynical." They live "whatever." They die young—emotionally, anyway, if not physically. They have empty eyes.

But what if you said, "I want to be like Jesus"? What if you started walking like Him, talking like Him? What if you started loving like Him?

What if, when you walked down the hall between classes, you heard people whispering, ". . . like Jesus"?

What if people started hanging around just because being near you made them happy, made them feel safe?

That could be you. You in Him; He in you. See you; see Him. The ultimate hero worship.

Be what you see.

Appendix 2

Using the Word in Worship

On her way back to God a few years ago, my sister decided to start going to church again. After a few weeks she called me, very annoyed. "What's going on?" she asked me. "Don't churches use the Bible anymore? The pastor talks for only 10 minutes, and I don't think he even takes a Bible to the pulpit. He sure doesn't preach from it. There's a responsive reading projected on a screen, but I don't know if it's from the Bible. Is this a church? Where's the Bible?"

There are still thousands of fine pastors who "preach the word" and "reprove, rebuke, exhort, with great patience and instruction." However, a growing number cater to those who "will not endure sound doctrine" and want "to have their ears tickled," who "turn away their ears from the truth" and "turn aside to myths" (2 Tim. 4:2-4, NASB).

One pastor friend of mine who rarely uses more than one text in a sermon justified this by saying, "Jesus taught by telling stories, and so do I." People love stories. So do I. Pastors can teach important lessons in memorable ways through the use of parables, but the fact is that they aren't Jesus, and what is more, their stories seldom offer the systematic biblical teaching so much needed by those in the pews whose mission is to "preach the gospel" to the world around them (Matt. 28:18-20). Many pastors offer baby food when what is needed is something solid (1 Cor. 3:1-3; Eph. 4:11-14).

We need to be thorough students of the Bible, knowing it, immersing ourselves in it, loving and treasuring it above all worldly things. It should be our joy, our meat and drink. Yet those of us who still carry our precious Bibles to church sometimes have no occasion to open them, even during the lesson study. This is a travesty, a horrible error keeping us from "the knowledge of God" (2 Cor. 10:5, NASB)—even though we may think we know Him and may claim to know Him.

Whatever our "itching ears" may *want* to hear, what we *need* to hear are carefully crafted expository sermons, revealing the meaning of long passages. We need thorough sermons on important biblical topics, drawn from texts throughout the Bible. A series on the fundamental beliefs of the church, explaining the scriptural support for each one, would be invaluable.

What I most long to see, though, is careful and prolonged reading of the Word of God—chapters, whole books, read straight through in church with occasional commentary on difficult verses.

Paul tells us "the word of God is living and active and sharper than any two-edged sword, . . . and able to judge the thoughts and intentions of the heart" (Heb. 4:12, NASB). He tells Timothy the Scriptures "are able to give you the wisdom that leads to salvation" (2 Tim. 3:15, NASB) and cautions him to rightly divide "the word of truth" (2 Tim. 2:15). He tells us "all Scripture is inspired by God and profitable for teaching, for reproof, for correction, for training in righteousness" (2 Tim. 3:16, NASB). Jesus told the Sadducees the reason they erred in their biblical interpretation was that they did not know the Scriptures (Matt. 22:29).

If these things are true, and they are, then why are we messing about in the pulpit with parables we've invented and anecdotes and funny stories? Why are we amusing the saints instead of training them?

There's another important aspect to this. Do the saints assemble to be entertained, to be marginally edified, to be educated, or to worship? If we dare answer the latter, then we would do well to consider what that means.

From the Psalms and from the hymns of Revelation we learn that the primary *purpose* of worship, of ascribing "worth-ship" to God (to return to the meaning of the original Old English word), is to praise God for His love, His justice, His mercy, His deliverance,

His mighty acts, His salvation. The primary *method* of worship is praise through testimony, through fervent congregational singing, and through prayer. A secondary purpose of worship is supplication through prayer.

One could argue that announcements, children's stories, special music, perhaps offerings, and even preaching are not really worship, because they are aimed primarily not at God but at the worshipers!

Do we worship a silent God? Is worship only about our talking to God, or is it also about God's talking to us? We might answer, with the Quakers, that God speaks wordlessly to our hearts, to our spirits, impresses us, moves us, if we are open to being moved. But is there more? There is. Ideally, preaching is God's response to His people's worship, and God has often reached me through preaching, but in too much preaching I do not sense God's voice (Rom. 10:14; 2 Tim. 4:2).

If we want to hear God speak to us in words, then we need to hear God's Word! Jesus says, of the Scriptures, "it is these that bear witness of Me" (John 5:39, NASB). If we want to know the Word, we need to know His word.

When the Israelites heard God's voice at Sinai, they begged Moses to ask God to be silent—He was too frightening. By marginalizing the Bible in our worship services, are we again asking God to be silent? Do our pastors take the place of Moses for us as they offer parables or platitudes in place of the voice of God, read aloud (Matt. 23:2)?

I have a dream—a dream of worshiping a God enthroned in the midst of His holy ones, a dream of worshiping a God who speaks, a dream of worship dominated by the Word of God.

Here is a radical proposal. What if once or twice a month, or even nearly every week, we returned to the primary biblical model, used in the synagogue, used by Jesus in Nazareth: the reading of Scripture as the center of worship, as God's response to our worship, with commentary to explain it when necessary (but with that commentary clearly secondary to the reading of God's Word)?

Not all pastors are capable of developing and delivering a great sermon, but they should all be able to read the Scriptures aloud, and given a bit of training they could learn to do it well. Many small churches depend on a local elder for most sermons. This is quite a burden (for all involved, sometimes), yet most elders would find reading Scripture aloud easier and more life-changing than preaching.

Surely one of the great occasions in the early church must have been the arrival of a letter from Paul or Peter or some other apostle. Surely much of the service must have been devoted to reading these revelations from God through humans. Surely they must have been read over and over.

Imagine a church service in which instead of a sermon the people heard an entire letter to Titus or Timothy or the Thessalonians, or a large part of a longer letter, or an entire book from the minor prophets, such as Amos or Micah. Praise, reproof, teaching, doctrine would be combined in a God-inspired order. Imagine the chastened hearts, the call to repentance and transformation.

If the congregation insists on hearing sermons every week, why couldn't lengthy readings from Scripture be part of every service? How about a chapter each week from each of the following: the Law, the Psalms, the Prophets, the Gospels, and the Epistles? Would five chapters of the Bible be too much for us to bear?

Thank God, my sister joined a church an hour's drive from her home where God's word is proclaimed and the members surround her with love. How many others like her, though, have turned away because they could not in good conscience attend a church where the Bible is not read? How many of us hesitate to bring Christian friends to our church because our pastor is "a good preacher" who holds the attention, but doesn't "preach the word"?

God's word, rightly read, will cut us to the core, break us open, expose us to the healing beams of the Sun of righteousness. It will lead us to radical surrender and transformation and service. It isn't soft and sentimental—it's a harsh medicine at times—but it's effective in preparing us for that consummation we so devoutly desire: Christ's soon return.

A Postscript: Tips on Effective Bible Reading

How can your congregation's hunger for the word be satisfied? Easy. Stand up and read! But there are ways of preparing for this reading that will make it clearer, more compelling. These techniques are easy to learn and easy to teach to others.

Don't read like this. You don't have to read the Bible like a Shakespearean actor might, with rolling thunder, moans, and gasps. In fact, such a reading draws attention to the beauty of the voice rather than freeing the Holy Spirit to draw the heart to the Father. Definitely avoid what I call the "high church Anglican" voice, heard in every cathedral in England—a high, clear, lisping tenor, effete and emotionless.

It doesn't matter if you have an Alabama drawl or a Nebraska twang. You don't have to project or support your diaphragm. Bass or soprano doesn't matter. What is ideal is that you disappear so that God's Word can be heard as directly as possible.

Which version? One of the problems with our present multiplicity of Bible versions is the difficulty of following along when someone reads from the Word. This was not a problem in Jesus' day, of course, because then one person read and the others listened. I find that despite the benefits of the "Berean" approach of reading along in one's own Bible, such reading can distract as one underlines or notices differences between versions or marginal references. Reading along may keep the mind busy enough to keep the Holy Spirit from breaking through to a submissive heart. So it might not be a bad idea to suggest that people close their Bibles and listen.

I myself like to read from the *New American Standard Bible*. I like its accuracy, even though the sentences are often long and complex and challenging to communicate, and I like its closeness to the KJV. The King James Version is beautiful, but the language is deliberately stately, much more so than the original Greek or Hebrew, or even than Tyndale's translation, on which the KJV is heavily based. The result is that it's very hard not to read it with a "liturgical voice." I think this detracts from the effective communication of the meaning and the Spirit. The New King James Version is excellent. The Revised Standard Version is accurate, but less graceful than most— the related New Revised Standard Version and Revised English Version both read better. The New International Version is less literal than those above, in general, but it reads very well aloud.

Preparation. Preparing to communicate God's Word through reading it aloud is not much different from preparing an expository sermon. You need to know the text just as thoroughly, but you share your insights through pause and emphasis rather than commentary and anecdotes. Here are five steps to follow:

1. *Pray.* First, pray that the Holy Spirit will illuminate the Word, guide you into truth, and keep you from misunderstanding.

2. *Read.* Read the chapters over and over until you understand them as well as possible. Be sure you understand the context, whether that be "who is speaking to whom under what circumstances" or the wider cultural or political context.

3. *Identify difficulties.* Note which passages seem confusing and give them extra time. With prayer and repetition, what seems cloudy at first often grows clear.

4. *Compare.* Compare your understanding of the chapters with that found in a couple good commentaries that don't take a skeptical approach to the Bible, but deal carefully with the words in the original language. Often these commentaries will answer your questions, and they will help you avoid misinterpretations you may have come up with on your own.

5. *Oral interpretation.* Return to the text and study out ways to communicate the meaning simply by the way you read. If you need to interrupt a long reading to explain something confusing, that's acceptable, but most of the explaining can be done by the way you read. There are two easy techniques for doing this:

A. *Emphasis.* Ac-*cent*-u-ate important words. Sometimes these words may be key terms or nouns or verbs, but sometimes they may be pronouns or conjunctions such as "and" or "but." The words you accentuate can reveal truths that have eluded your listeners.

B. *Pause.* One. Two. There are words and phrases in the Bible of such importance that listeners need extra time to process them. If you rush on, you may stymie the Spirit's work. It is up to you, though, to discover where these pauses are needed. Commas, colons, and periods all indicate pauses of different lengths. You should take advantage of these guides, but look for places where longer pauses might be needed.

It may be useful to photocopy the chapters you plan to read, then mark the accents and pauses. You might, say, highlight in yellow the words you want to accent and place a red slash where a significant pause is needed.

An Example. Here's an example of what accents and pauses can reveal about Isaiah 53:4, 5. First, here's the way the passage is usually read, from the NIV:

"Surely he took up our **infirmities**
  and **carried** our **sorrows,**
  Yet we considered him stricken by **God,**
  smitten by him, and **afflicted.**
  But he was **pierced** for our **transgressions,**
  he was **crushed** for our **iniquities;**
  the **punishment** that brought us **peace** was **upon** him,
  and by his **wounds** we are **healed.**"

This emphasizes primarily nouns and verbs, reminding us of what would happen to the Messiah. Note, though, the effect of accentuating primarily the pronouns:

"Surely **he** took up **our** infirmities
  and carried **our** sorrows,//
  Yet **we** considered him **stricken by God,**//

163

smitten by him,// and **afflicted.**//
But **he** was pierced for **our** transgressions,//
he was crushed for **our** iniquities;//
the **punishment** that brought **us peace** was upon **him,**//
and by **his** wounds **we** are healed."

Now, without any need for your comments, your listeners will understand that this prophecy reveals that the Messiah's death would be a substitutionary atonement, the antitype of the tabernacle sacrifices. You could drive home this point by commenting that the "peace" mentioned refers to the "peace offering."

Both readings are valid, in this case, but the second is, I think, more illuminating. It reminds us, in an emotionally devastating way, that Christ died for each of us, that each of us is responsible for His death.

Slow down! Even if you are called upon to read the Scriptures publicly without time for preparation, there is one important thing you can do to help God's Word live in the minds of your listeners: slow down. We tend to read the Bible far too fast for the Spirit to move us and help us comprehend.

I tried timing myself while reading aloud from John 18, Isaiah 53, and 1 Corinthians 7. First I tried reading them at the speed they are generally read aloud, and found that my speed varied from 160 to 184 words per minute. Then I read them again, this time at a speed calculated to increase understanding, pausing at appropriate places. This time I read from 102 to 125 words per minute, with the slowest speed for the poetry in Isaiah. Thus I would recommend that the best reading speed is about 70 percent of your usual speed.

Do it. This may sound like a lot of work, but it's certainly no harder than preparing a good sermon, and you'll gain a blessing from your time in the Word. Give it a try. Watch the congregation as you read. Watch tears running down cheeks as people hear God's Word again and experience the Holy Spirit's sweet rain, bringing conviction and encouragement.

Appendix 3

"Sabbath Is a Happy Day!"

What Does Isaiah 58:13 and 14 Mean?

The primary focus of this book has been Christian music, both for personal use and for congregational use. Considering music in the worship service has led in turn to looking at the rest of the church service, the characteristics of those who come to worship, and how to incorporate the reading of Scripture into worship. But we don't spend the entire day in church. What should we do with the rest of the Sabbath, this precious gift from God to humanity? In this chapter we will look carefully at one of the most important Bible passages on this topic.

I recently gave a weekend seminar on biblical topics for a group of seventy young people in what is considered the most conservative part of Germany—an area where the ideas about music found in this book are considered controversial. Given their conservative reputation, I was shocked when after Sabbath dinner the students and the conference youth director rushed outside and spent a couple sweaty hours playing soccer and volleyball.[1] This was not considered acceptable Sabbath observance when (and where) I was a boy.

God's call in Isaiah 58:13, 14 for us to avoid "doing your pleasure" (verse 13, NKJV) on the Sabbath resonates with us, but what does it mean?

---

[1] A friend of mine on a speaking tour with Samuele Bacchiocchi was similarly surprised, some years ago, to find this champion of the Sabbath playing soccer on Sabbath afternoon with a group of theology students at Villa Aurora, near Florence, Italy. Ideas of acceptable behavior are culturally based, and evidently in Germany and Italy what is acceptable differs from American standards. We need to learn to tolerate such differences, rather than condemning them out of hand.

Many denominations over the centuries have at times had strict rules against "Sabbathbreaking," though they've defined it in various ways, whether carrying a purse, attending plays, purchasing liquor, or mowing the lawn.[2]

Have they been correct in this? Generations of young people have found the Sabbath a burden and moaned about the many pleasures forbidden them on that day.[3] Just how happy a day should the Sabbath be?

The fourth commandment does not forbid pleasure on Sabbath, but only work. The Hebrew word translated "you shall labor," *ta‘ᵃbōd,* is "sweat of your brow" work, like that done by an *‘ebed,* a servant or slave. The Hebrew word translated "your work," *mᵉla’k-ttekā,* especially suggests occupations, such as shopkeeper or artisan, the work of commerce, though it also means all work.[4] The Old Testament says very little about Sabbath worship, but it strongly emphasizes Sabbath rest. The Hebrew word for Sabbath, *šabbat,* is a noun. The verb it is derived from, *šabat,* means "to cease," primarily from work.

Most of Isaiah 58 deals with fasting as practiced, versus fasting as God wishes it do be practiced.[5] In verse 3 God mocks the people for wondering why he doesn't seem to see them fasting, but he has seen them serving their own interests by oppressing their workers on their fast days. I see 4a, "Look, you fast only to quarrel and to fight and to strike with a wicked fist," as parallel to 3b: "Look, you serve your own

---

[2] See, for example, the tractate Shabbat in the Mishnah.

[3] I dedicate this article to my 14-year-old son Paul, whose frequent question "What's wrong with doing it on Sabbath?" encouraged me to search the Scriptures.

[4] F. Brown, S. Driver, and C. Briggs, *Hebrew and English Lexicon* (Peabody, Mass: Hendrickson [1906], 1996), pp. 521, 522.

[5] The only fast day required by the Torah, of course, is on the Day of Atonement. On this basis, Roy Gane suggests that the fast day in question may actually be the Day of Atonement (personal e-mail). On this day, one recalls, not only is fasting required, but work is forbidden. By this light, the Sabbath in verses 13 and 14 is not the weekly Sabbath but the ceremonial Sabbath of the Day of Atonement. Actually, this would tie the chapter together very effectively. The problem is that it would suggest that it is only on the Day of Atonement that God desires service to those in need.

166

interest on your fast day, and oppress all your workers" (NRSV).

Thus the quarreling and fighting and striking "with a wicked fist" should be seen as actions *against oppressed workers,* not against, say, neighbors. Serving "your own interest" is closely connected here with this oppression of workers in order to maximize profits, so we should see it as having something to do with employment, not with pleasure or entertainment.

The Sabbath Promise

Often Sabbath pleasures are denied on the basis of one of the loveliest promises in the Bible, Isaiah 58:13, 14, which reads, in the New King James Version,

"If you turn away your foot from the Sabbath,
From doing your pleasure on My holy day,
And call the Sabbath a delight,
The holy day of the Lord honorable,
And shall honor Him, not doing your own ways,
Nor finding your own pleasure,
Nor speaking your own words,
Then you shall delight yourself in the Lord;
And I will cause you to ride on the high hills of the earth,
And feed you with the heritage of Jacob your father.
The mouth of the Lord has spoken."

This is quite a literal translation, but when I read it some questions come to mind. Answering those questions will help us understand what God is really saying through his prophet. If we let it, the Bible will be its own interpreter.

The Delight of Sabbath

Let's move now to our text. God asks us to call the Sabbath a delight. I assume that when we say that, we should be telling the truth. That means learning to find it delightful, or doing on it what is delightful.

The Hebrew word translated "delight," found twice in verses 13 and 14, is 'oneg, which means "exquisite delight," "dainty," "soft," and "delicate."[6] It sometimes refers to luxury, what is rich and delicious, like Sabbath dinner. That's God's intention for the Sabbath! It should be the most exquisite, luxuriously delightful day of the week! Isn't that better than "your own pleasure"? But if the Sabbath is an "exquisite delight" for us, are we not taking pleasure in it?

In verse 14, 'oneg is in what Hebrew scholars call the Hithpael form, tit'annag. Words in the Hithpael form are usually reflexive, meaning what one does to oneself. "Delight yourself" is a good translation. Brown, Drivers, and Briggs translate the word as "take exquisite delight."

However, the same word is found in Isaiah 57:4, and the BDB says that usage means to "make merry over." Does this suggest it's OK to make merry on the Sabbath, to be lighthearted, to laugh? Perhaps, even though the context is quite different. Can you imagine Jesus laughing on Sabbath? I can. A merry heart can heal the spirit, after all (Proverbs 17:22), and Jesus approves of healing on the Sabbath (Matt. 12:10-12).

Textual Questions

"From the Sabbath." Let's look now at some of the questions raised by the text. The first question stems from the faulty parallelism introduced by the translators: "If you turn away your foot from the Sabbath, . . . and call the Sabbath a delight . . ." If we turn away our feet from the Sabbath, why would we call the Sabbath a delight? As translated, this makes no sense.

However, the answer to this question is easy. In Hebrew, the phrase "from the Sabbath" is one word, mišabbat. That mi is short for min, which is usually translated "from." Several dozen times, how-

---

[6] Brown, Drivers, and Briggs, p. 772.

ever, it means not "from," but "on account of," or "because of." That's the correct translation here, as well.[7]

For example, in Isaiah 53:5, *min* is usually translated "for," meaning "on account of." The first phrase can be translated, "He was pierced because of our transgressions." That's *min!*

So the text is talking about turning away from something "on account of" the Sabbath, because observing the Sabbath requires this turning away. It doesn't mean turning away "from" the Sabbath.[8]

"Turn away." Second, what does it mean to "turn away your foot"? Does it mean to stop trampling on the Sabbath? No, it doesn't. It's an idiomatic expression.

"Turning away the foot" means stopping whatever one is doing and returning to where one came from. The Hebrew word translated "turn away" is related to the Hebrew word *shūb,* "return." This is God's Old Testament word for repentance.

(The New Living Translation uses the wonderful phrase "turn away from sin and toward God" when it translates the New Testament word usually translated as "repent.")

It's interesting, though, that the Hebrew word is in the form called the Hiphil. Words in the Hiphil form usually refer to causing something. The BDB translates this word as "cause to return."[9] It might also mean "bring back" or "draw back."

The important thing to note, though, is what the Hiphil form used here tells us. Turning away from our daily activities and returning to Sabbathkeeping is our own choice. It's not automatic, it's not a forced decision, and it's not an accident. God asks us to make that choice.

Sabbath pleasures? Third, what is meant by "your own plea-

---

[7] Green's *Literal Translation of the Holy Bible* renders the clause, "If you turn your foot away *because of* the Sabbath."

[8] The Jewish Publication Society translation called *Tanakh* renders the clause, "If you refrain from trampling the sabbath." The Israelites were indeed trampling the Sabbath, but this translation neglects the idiomatic expression "turn your foot away," which is not related to trampling.

[9] Brown, Drivers, and Briggs, p. 998.

sure"? What does that include? If we take delight in the Sabbath, isn't that pleasure?

Studying the passage in Hebrew has led me to believe that "pleasure" and "idle words" are not what Isaiah meant when he delivered his message from God. There is another valid way of translating the verses that better fits the fourth commandment's prohibition of work on the seventh day.

"Pleasure" is the most common meaning of the Hebrew noun *ḥepeṣ,* but not the only meaning. A form of *ḥepeṣ* is used twice in verse 13. It also appears in verse 3, where it is tied to the exploitation of employees.

I think the English translators chose "finding your own pleasure" because it contrasted nicely with the true "delight" we should find in the Sabbath. They thought the verse was saying, "Don't do what pleases you, but what pleases God." Such parallels often exist in the Hebrew text, but not here, I think.

So what else might the noun *ḥepeṣ* mean besides "pleasure"? The word also means "business," "affair," and "matter." It occurs in Ecclesiastes 3:1 and 17, in the phrase "a time for every purpose" (NKJV), which we never translate as "a time for every pleasure." Indeed, Brown, Drivers, and Briggs even gives "doing thy affairs" as the preferred translation in Isaiah 58:13, rather than "doing your pleasure."[10]

Thus God is not speaking against pleasure here, but against working, doing business on Sabbath. "Finding your own pleasure" should actually be translated "finding business," or "looking for customers."

Silence on Sabbath? Fourth, in the NKJV italicized words are not in the original. "Nor speaking *your own* words" reads, literally, not "speaking words." Are we to remain silent on the Sabbath? The New International Version changes this to not "speaking idle words," which makes sense, but it's not what the Hebrew says.

In Hebrew, the expression is *davēr dāvār,* "the speaking of a

---

[10] *Ibid.,* p. 343.

word." Is God asking for silence on Sabbath? No, He's not. The noun *dāvār* is usually translated "word," as in "the word of the Lord, but it seldom means an actual word. It's more likely to mean a "statement," a "message," a "speech," a "report," an "edict," or even a "thing."

However, more significantly, *dāvār* sometimes means a "matter" or "affair" or "business" or "occupation."[11] In 1 Samuel 21:8 it's translated "business." In 2 Samuel 19:29 we also find the words *davēr . . . dāvār*. There they are translated "speak . . . of your matters" (NKJV), as in "business matters."

We find, thus, that God is asking us to refrain not only from "finding business," but from "talking business" or making deals on Sabbath. Does this mean that if I invite people over for lunch on Sabbath, I shouldn't ask them how their work is going? I don't think so. But spending the afternoon discussing work does not fill us with delight. It isn't refreshing.

Does this mean it's now OK to "speak idle words," to talk about nothing? I don't think it's a good idea. But it's not what this passage is actually prohibiting.

"Doing your own ways." Fifth, we're familiar with the phrase "going your own way," but both the Hebrew and the NKJV read *"doing* your own ways." This is peculiar.

The Hebrew word *derek* usually means "road" or "way." When Enoch walked with God, he walked on God's road, going God's way, because that's where God walks. If we go our own way, we are not on God's road. But the verb here is not *"going* your own way," but *"doing* your own ways."

"Doing" your way or road doesn't make sense, so we should look for another meaning of *derek*. We find the word also means what is "customary," our usual "undertaking" or way of doing business.[12] So, again the text speaks against working on Sabbath, this time not against "finding" or "talking," but against "doing."

---

[11] *Ibid.,* p. 183.
[12] *Ibid.,* p. 203.

What Does This Mean?

"Finding your own pleasure" actually means "finding business," looking for potential customers. "Speaking words" actually means "talking business." "Doing your own ways" actually means "doing business as usual."

Translating these phrases this way fits nicely with the fourth commandment, as well, as it forbids both field labor and commerce.

But was working on Sabbath a serious problem for the Israelites? Wasn't the Sabbath always precious to them? Nehemiah writes, in Nehemiah 13:15, "In those days I saw men in Judah treading wine-presses on the Sabbath and bringing in grain and loading it on donkeys, together with wine, grapes, figs and all other kinds of loads. And they were bringing all this into Jerusalem on the Sabbath. Therefore I warned them against selling food on that day" (NIV).

Was this happening in Isaiah's time, as well? In verse 18 Nehemiah says, "Didn't your forefathers do the same things, so that our God brought all this calamity upon us and upon this city?" In Isaiah 58, God is trying to get those forefathers to avoid the coming catastrophe by putting aside their daily work and not treating the Sabbath as a normal business day.

Are there any Bible versions that have realized this passage is speaking against doing business on Sabbath? Yes, there are several: Goodspeed, the Berkeley Version, the New English Bible, the Tanakh, and the Jerusalem Bible. I was pleased to find, after doing this word study, that I wasn't alone in this understanding of the text.

A Revised Version

There's a lot more to discover in these verses, but I think I can now propose a very literal translation from the Hebrew that more accurately expresses both God's will and the meaning of the text.

I've repeated one implied word ("day") for the sake of clarity. Other than that, every word is a literal translation of the Hebrew original. The word order is as close to the original as possible.

If you turn back, on account of the Sabbath,
Your foot's doing of your affairs on my holy day,
And you call to the Sabbath, "Exquisite delight!"
To the holy *day* of Yahweh, "Honored!"
And if you make it honorable,
Without[13] doing your customary undertaking,
Without finding your business
And talking of business,
Then you will take exquisite delight in Yahweh,
And I will make you ride over the high places of the land,
And I will make you eat of the inheritance of Jacob your father,
Because the mouth of Yahweh has spoken.

The passage doesn't mean "Don't do what you please on Sabbath." It means "Don't do what you please if what pleases you is working." Remember too that the Sabbath is not only a deliverance from work, but a symbol of deliverance from our own works.

This doesn't mean Sabbath is for doing whatever we feel like doing. But *pleasure* is not forbidden. Luxurious delight and a merry heart are not forbidden. If it is not our ordinary work, if it delights us, and if we can share that delight with God without rationalizing our behavior, then God smiles on us.

Conversely, if what we do makes the Sabbath a misery to us or to our children, if it makes us hate Sabbath, if it makes us long for Sabbath to be over, we're going the wrong way. In a sense, whatever we do on Sabbath that is not delightful in a God-honoring way breaks the Sabbath.

Now that we realize it is not pleasure God prohibits on Sabbath but business, perhaps more of us will experience its "delicate delight." I remember singing, as a child, "Sabbath is a happy day!" It should be.

---

[13] "Without" is one of many possible translations of the Hebrew word *min*. The main idea of *min* is *separation*. In Job 11:15, "without spot," and Proverbs 1:33, "without fear," the Hebrew word translated "without" is *min* (*ibid.,* pp. 577, 578, especially 1.b).